UNFINISHED ROAD TO JUSTICE

TENGIMPILO MAQEBHULA

CONTENTS

As THIS BOOK IS A true story and narrates the painful stories and days in my life, I wish to acknowledge the unwavering support displayed by my wife Sindisiwe Maqebhula, my late mother Masotshantshi Qakaza Maqebhula and my in-laws, the Hlamvu family, who guided me with prayers during the era of the "Reign of Terror".

The moral, spiritual and emotional support from some of officers of the Division Forensic Services: Criminal Record and Crime Scene Management SAPS Eastern Cape will never be forgotten: Colonel Nobhuzana, former Colonel Mphalo, Lt Colonel Gelese, former Lt Colonel Lila, Captain Bungu, Lubabalo Ndingane, members of the Local Criminal Record Centre Grahamstown and junior members of the South African Police Service in Grahamstown.

PREFACE

Unfinished Road to Justice DESCRIBES the disillusionment of a former commander in the South African Police, Tengimpilo Maqebhula, with the justice system, as he and many other black and coloured police officers have been subject to unfair practices. Maqebhula was a commander from 2004 to 2024 in the following areas: Cradock in the Karoo area and Grahamstown, now under the Sara Baartman District.

His experience was that the decisions to prosecute or not to prosecute officers depended on the colour of their skin. He experienced a lot of injustices and inequalities before the law and in disciplinary processes. Over the years, he witnessed the criminal charging of coloured and black people and police officers, including himself, by the Grahamstown Deputy Director of Public Prosecutions office for offences never committed. In many instances, they were found not guilty and discharged in terms of Section 174 of the Criminal Procedure Act, 1977.

This abuse of power or perceived racism is self-evident in the lawsuits (civil claims) for malicious prosecution against the Justice and Police Departments in these areas. During these years, he exposed painful incidents where black and coloured police were treated and subjected to criminal and disciplinary processes and subsequently dismissed from work for offences that did not exist. On the other hand, he exposed how some white police who committed serious cases were protected by the system and are still working in the police.

As he reported all these atrocities, he was persecuted and subjected to criminal and departmental investigations for the rest of his career as commander. His attempt to approach the Port Elizabeth Labour Court for protection as a whistle blower in terms of Protected Disclosure Act, 2000, as amended, could not stop the victimisation and harassment by the South African Police authorities.

As he represented a number of police in disciplinary matters and arbitrations, he managed to interview and document the painful stories of those dismissed police officers. He also exposed these atrocities to the media, and took their cases of unlawful and unconstitutional dismissal to the High Court of Grahamstown.

CHAPTER ONE

Arrival in Cradock and becoming a black commander over white police officers

As the then British Prime Minister Harold Macmillan said to the South African Parliament on the 3rd of February 1960, "The wind of change is blowing through this African continent. Whether we like it or not, this growth of national consciousness is a political fact."

In South Africa, after 1994 the winds of change continued to blow and as a result the South African Parliament passed most important legislation called the Employment Equity Act no 55 of 1998. That piece of law paved the way for transformation and addressing the imbalances of the pasts in the employment sector.

This historical act compelled the white management of the Criminal Record Centre of South African Police Service to appoint and promote junior black commanders to middle management positions. There was a lot of resistance by senior white police managers, who claimed that black managers were not capable of working as commanders or as fingerprints experts in the Criminal Record Centre. However, everything went ahead against them. At that time there was a lot of disillusionment and discontent amongst the white police officers.

This is where my book *Unfinished Road to Justice* starts. Myself and other black commanders were promoted to those positions, taking over from white commanders. I was promoted to Cradock, in the Karoo area, to the rank of captain, and became a commander over white police officers.

On my arrival, I noticed that, although South African Police policy on channels of communication directed that the lowest rank must report to the next higher rank on a daily basis – constable to sergeant, warrant officer to captain and so on – those white police officers under me bypassed me and reported directly to my commander, who was a white brigadier at the provincial level, and he allowed that.

I further noticed that disciplinary processes were only taken against black police officers and the white police officers were not subjected to disciplinary processes. While I was still noticing that practice, there came a big challenge that forced me to take steps against a white police officer. A criminal case of theft of petrol from a state vehicle was reported to me by garage owners in Cradock. They reported as follows: this member normally approached their garage assistants and instructed them to first put petrol in the state vehicle and to then put some into a five- or ten-litre container and swipe the state petrol card in a single payment.

As commander and accounting officer, I had a legal duty to open a criminal case and a departmental case of fraud against the member. As these state petrol cards were managed by the bank, I therefore requested the services of WesBank in terms of forensic investigation and the bank forensic investigator furnished me with the report and there was overwhelming evidence on the report that the petrol put into the containers was never put into the state vehicle.

An investigating officer was appointed by the Cradock branch commander for the case and he was a white captain. As I opened the case, I mentioned on the diary of the docket that I had a name list of witnesses from different garages who were the petrol attendants who were previously instructed by my staff member to put petrol in containers, and that the forensic reported was awaited.

It is procedure that, if a case docket is opened, an investigator must interview the complainant to get more information; in fact, not only in the police, but you have to consult and interview the person who lodges a complaint. It never happened to me, although we were working in the same police station with the investigating officer. I only got an informal report that the case had been referred to the Grahamstown deputy director of the Public Prosecutions office for a decision, and they had declined to prosecute. On my side, I was waiting for the investigating officer to interview me, but no-one every came.

It is also a procedure that, if a criminal case is opened against a police officer, a decision to prosecute or not will be taken by the National Prosecuting Authority in Grahamstown, which is the head office of the Eastern Cape judiciary, but a full investigation must still take place at the particular place where it was reported.

CHAPTER TWO

Beginning to report unethical behaviours in the justice system to the authorities

I REPORTED THIS MALADMINISTRATION TO the area commissioner, raising the question of how come an empty docket with no statements and no investigation can simply be taken for decision, but the matter could not go any further. Instead, I was informed by other black police officers that it was a normal practice in those areas.

If a case was opened against a white police officer or a white person, white state advocates in Grahamstown National Prosecuting Authority would be the first to know. They would directly phone the investigating officer and pressure him to bring the docket for decision, and this was a normal practice for all offices that fall under Grahamstown Head Office: offices like Middleburg, Graaff Reinette, Jeffreys Bay, Cradock, Bedford, Queenstown, Hofmeyer, Somerset East and others.

It became clear that the then area commissioner had no authority over decisions of state prosecutors and advocates, so I reported the matter to the deputy director of Public Prosecutions in Grahamstown. The nature of my complaint was about the alleged conduct of white investigating officers who brought an empty docket, and the conduct of that white state advocate who received an empty docket and decided to take a decision without their being any statements. I made references to the case numbers where the white police officers were the suspects.

My complaint was informed by my experience of more than fifteen years working with state prosecutors and state advocates in Mthatha, in my capacity as investigating officer. According to my experience, where the state prosecutors noticed that more information was needed, they would give you instructions to go and get more information and obtain more statements before they made any decisions.

I never got an answer. Instead, I was subjected to a series of departmental and criminal investigations and it became clear that my commander – who was a white brigadier to whom I also reported many cases of misconduct by white police officers in my office, which he ignored – was at the centre of the persecutions and victimisation.

The matter was so serious that my dairies and the vehicle registers of the vehicle I used to drive went missing and I opened up a criminal case of theft of official documents as Grahamstown cas 329/12/2010.

At that time I was promoted from Cradock to Grahamstown, but victimisation followed me and I was charged with more than thirty-five charges and a notice of suspension without pay was served on me. After a year, a disciplinary officer, who was tasked by this white brigadier as an employer representative for my departmental case, furnished me with documentation so as to prepare the case.

While pursuing them, I noticed that copies of those stolen documents as per Grahamstown cas 329/12/2010 were filed as evidence against me, and the complainant was my commander, that white brigadier. As I was subjected to daily investigations, my juniors, who were white, were following me day and night to see where I was going and reporting directly to the brigadier, in contravention of South African Police Regulations in terms of channels of communication. In terms of my provincial office structure, my commander was the provincial head. Under him there were two black colonels, but these white junior police officers were reporting directly to that brigadier.

I reported all these issues to the offices of the Provincial Commissioner and National Commissioner, but they were simply closed without any investigation. In fact, I did furnish them with evidence and documentation that the copies of stolen documents as per Grahamstown cas 329/12/2010 were found in possession of that brigadier and the colonels were going to be witness to the effect that they got those stolen documents from him. One colonel had been tasked to certify them as a true copy and another was given those copies of documents to be handed to me.

CHAPTER THREE

Labour Court application and referral

As I COULD NOT GET any help from police commissioners, I took my complaint of victimisation to Labour court for protection as a whistle-blower in terms of the Protected Disclosure Act, read with the Labour Act on victimisation as follows:

IN THE LABOUR COURT OF SOUTH AFRICA HELD IN PORT ELIZABETH

Case no P 377/12

In the matter between
TENGIMPILO MAQEBHULA APPLICANT
And

THE MINSTER OF SAFETY AND SECURITY FIRST RESPONDENT
THE NATIONAL COMMISSIONER OF THE
SOUTH AFRICA POLICE SERVICE SECOND RESPONDENT
BRIGADIER BOTHA THIRD RESPONDENT

Unfair Labour Practice as contemplated by Section 186(2) (d) of the Labour Relations Act no 66 of 1995 (herein referred to as "LRA"). Namely

"...an occupational detriment, other than dismissal, in contravention of the Protected Disclosures Act, 2000 ... on account of the employee having made a protected disclosure in terms of the Act.

ALTERNATIVELY:

as contemplated by section 5 (2) (c) of the Labour Relations Act, more particularly, without limiting the general protection conferred by sub section (1), no person may do, or threaten to do any of the following – Prejudice an employee because of the past, present, or anticipated; Exercise of any right conferred by this Act, or participation in any proceedings in terms of this Act...

I therefore I acted in terms of 191 (13), which affords employees a choice of referring an unfair labour practice to the Labour Court for adjudication. As I was subjected to an occupational detriment by my employer, I referred the matter to the CCMA and the CCMA referred the case to the Labour Court.

In my statement of claim I submitted that, between 2008 and 2009, until 2011, I'd reported the acts of maladministration, cover ups and perceived racism by the Criminal Record Centre provincial commander. As a result of that, I was subjected to criminal and departmental investigations. It was my further submission that even my annual leave was not approved and it was against this background that I sought the intervention of the Labour Court. I was also not allowed to attend union meetings, although I was the national chairperson of the Police Union.

IN THE LABOUR COURT OF SOUTH AFRICA

HELD AT PORT ELIZABETH

CASE NO : P377/12

In the matter between:

T MAQEBHULA   **APPLICANT**

and

THE MINISTER OF SAFETY AND SECURITY   **FIRST RESPONDENT**

THE NATIONAL COMMISSIONER OF THE   **SECOND RESPONDENT**
SOUTH AFRICAN POLICE SERVICES

BRIGADIER BOTHA   **THIRD RESPONDENT**

STATEMENT OF CLAIM

STATEMENT OF CASE:

1. The Applicant will accept notices and service of all documents in this
    matter at the address of Messrs Brown Braude & Vlok Inc as set
    hereunder:

    317 Cape Road
    Newton Park
    Port Elizabeth
    6065

Letter unlawfully disallowing me from attending union activities dated 2014/11/01

Private Bag   X 7471 King William's Town   Fax   043 604 6306

                                                                   086 515 3931

YOUR REFERENCE   THE PROVINCIAL HEAD

REFERENCE: 4/1/3   SOUTH AFRICAN POLICE SERVICE

ENQUIRIES: BRIGADIER BOTHA   CRIMINAL RECORD AND CRIME SCENE MANAGEMENT

TEL: 043 604 6305   EASTERN CAPE

                                        KING WILLIAM'S TOWN

                                        2014-11-02

The Commander   Attention: Lt Col Maqebhula
SAPS
Local Criminal Record Centre
GRAHAMSTOWN

SHORPSTERWARDS:TERMINATION OF OFFICE:NO 0490165-7 LT COL MAQEBHULA

1. This office has been informed that you are still actively involved as a shop steward within the Public Service Association.

2. In terms of paragraph 10.1 (annexure D) of procedural agreement 3/2005, a shop steward shall cease to hold office when promoted to level 9.

3. As a Commander of Local Criminal Record Centre, Grahamstown, at salary level 10, your involvement as a shop steward is in contravention of said SSSBC agreement and in conflict with your responsibilities as a commander.

4. It is hereby directed that you terminate all shop steward activities with immediate effect.

5. Kindly acknowledge receipt hereof.

Kind regards

_________________________________   BRIGADIER
PROVINCIAL HEAD: CR&CSM: EASTERN CAPE
RH BOTHA

By the time I received this unlawful letter, dated 2014/11/01, I was the leader of that union and as their leader I had to visit places and give support to union members. But I could not stop because the Constitution of South Africa says "every person has a right to fair labour practice". SAPS legal service of the Eastern Cape hired the most senior advocates against me to defend a white brigadier who was victimising me on a daily basis and some R150 000 was paid just for consultation by SAPS.

And on the other side the National Prosecuting Authority of Grahamstown never responded to my complaint.

Surprisingly, I saw the purported response in the replying affidavit from the state attorney, who represented the South African Police. Paragraph 33.12 reads as follows

In response, the Director of Public Prosecutions Grahamstown, stated as follows on 15 January 2010:

Any suggestion that any member of my staff made the decision not to prosecute on the basis of perceived racial prejudice or discrimination is unbecoming and unsubstantiated. Captian Maqebhula would be well advised to refrain from personal attacks of this nature.

I was so surprised about these comments because I'd reported these incidents through a letter in 2008 and I never got a response from Grahamstown DPP's office. At the same time I received summons/indictment from the Grahamstown Deputy Director of Public Prosecuting Authority, summoning me to appear as the accused in the Cradock Magistrate Court.

It was another surprise because I never came across nor was approached by the investigating officer informing me about a case opened against me.

I requested an explanation as to what happened, and was informed that Mr Jacobus Goerge Kersop complained to the Grahamstown DPP's office and I appeared in Cradock.

Notice to appear/summons dated 27 December 2005 NPA Grahamstown

National Prosecution Service
Director of Public Prosecutions:
Eastern Cape

EASTERN CAPE
DIVISION

Grahamstown

Tel: +27 46 602 3000
Fax: +27 46 602 3062

94 High Street
GRAHAMSTOWN
6139

Private Bag X1009
GRAHAMSTOWN
6140
SOUTH AFRICA

www.npa.gov.za

Ref: 9/2/12-414/06
Enq: ADV. OBERMEYER
Date: 27 DECEMBER 2006

The Control Prosecutor
Private Bag X54
CRADOCK
5880

THE STATE VERSUS TENGIMPILO MAQEBHULA
YOUR 9/2/4/1 DATED 30 NOVEMBER 2006

1. Tengimpilo Maqebhula must be prosecuted in the Magistrate's Court on charges of:

   i) Contravening regulation 305(1)(a) of the National Road Traffic Regulations 2000 read with sections 1, 89(1) and 89(6) of Act 93 of 1996 (Parking a vehicle in contravention of a road traffic sign),

   ii) Contravening section 12(a) read with sections 1, 89(1) and 89(6) of Act 93 of 1996 (Driving a motor vehicle on a public road without a driver's licence); alternatively contravening section 12(b) read with sections 1, 89(1) and 89(6) of Act 93 of 1996 (Driving a motor vehicle on a public road without having his driver's licence in his vehicle),

   iii) Contravening section 3J(1)(a) read with sections 1, 3I(h), 89(1) and 89(6) of Act 93 of 1996 (Failing to comply with an instruction or direction of a traffic officer, to wit to supply his name and address) and

   (iv) Assault.

2. The case docket, Cradock CAS 19/9/2005, is enclosed.

3. Kindly report the date and result of the trial to this office, before 30 June 2007.

4. Despite my request dated 26 October 2006 and a telephonic discussion on 15 December 2006 between Adv. Obermeyer of my office and Mr. Jacobs, he has not supplied me with his report in relation to the decrease of the traffic fine nor with a copy of the control document and all correspondence in relation to the fine.

5. The report and other documents must be supplied immediately.

DIRECTOR OF PUBLIC PROSECUTIONS: EASTERN CAPE

CHAPTER FOUR

At the Magistrate Court as an accused person

TRIAL IN CRADOCK

IN THE MAGISTRATE'S COURT FOR EASTERN CAPE REGION

HELD AT:CRADOCK

CASE NO 89/06 DATE 15 November 2007

In the matter between

THE STATE VERSUS

TENGIMPILO MAQEBHULA ACCUSED

State case: Prosecutor

PROSECUTOR: Accused person Tengimpilo Maqebhula is representing himself and the matter is on the roll. The state is ready to proceed.

COURT: Are all your witness here?

PROSECUTOR: Your Worship, the witnesses are here.

COURT: All of them?

PROSECUTOR: Yes, they are, Your Worship.

COURT: All the witness that you are calling?

PROSECUTOR: There are only two.

ACCUSED: May I please, Your Worship, confirm that I represent myself and am ready to proceed.

COURT: You can proceed to put the matter to the accused.

PROSECUTOR: Case C 89/06 George Jacobus Kersop Versus Tengimpilo Maqebhula.

The Accused is the commander of Cradock Criminal Record Centre and is holding the rank of Captain. On 9 September 2005, at about 13h00, the accused unlawfully parked a state vehicle in a place designated for disabled persons and refused to take the instruction of the traffic officer.

The accused person is guilty of:

1. Count (1), contravening Regulation 305 (1) (a) of the National Traffic Act Regulations 2000 read Sections 89 (1) and 89 (6), of Act 93 of 1996 (parking a vehicle in contravention of a road traffic sign)
2. Count (2), contravening section 12 (a) read with Sections 1, 89 (1) and 89 (6) of Act 93 of 1996 (driving a motor vehicle on a public road without a driver's licence alternatively contravening Sections 12 (b) read with Sections 1, 89 (1) and 89 (6) of Act of 1996.
3. Count (3), contravening Section 3J (1) (a) read with Sections 1, 31(h), 89(1) and 89(6) of Act 93 of 1996 (failing to comply with an instruction or directive of a traffic officer, to wit to supply his name and address).
4. Count (4), assault.

COURT: You understand the charges?

ACCUSED: Yes, I understand.

COURT: How do you plea to the charges.

ACCUSED: Pleads not guilty and I reserve the plea explanation at this stage.

COURT: You may be seated. The State must proceed.

PROSECUTOR: I am now calling Mr George Jacobus Kersop as first witness.

COURT: What is your name?

WITNESS: George Jacobus Kersop.

COURT: Can you swear that whatever you are going to say in this court is the truth and nothing but the truth? If so, say so help me, God.

WITNESS: So help me, God.

PROSECUTOR: Can you tell this court what happened on this day in question?

WITNESS: on 9 September 2005, I was on duty as traffic officer and I was checking some vehicles that did not comply with road traffic laws and I was at Spar. I noticed a white car parked in the disabled parking. As it was too hot, I had removed my jacket that displayed my identification and my rank.

As the accused was sitting in the car, I knocked at the window of the car and I asked for his licence and he said, "Who are you?" He was starting the car and I noticed that he was reversing and I decided to forcefully grab the car keys and take them into my possession.

PROSECUTOR: Proceed.

WITNESS: He jumped out of the car and grabbed me, trying to take the keys back and in the process the gentleman assaulted me. The scuffle took place and Mr Mulluman, who is going to be the second witness, appeared and helped me. However, the gentleman managed to get his car keys back and he drove away.

I traced the gentleman and I was informed he is the new commander of Cradock Local Criminal Record Centre and I decided to open a case of assault and driving a vehicle without a driver's licence.

That is all that happened.

COURT: Accused, stand up. Do you have any questions for this witness?

ACCUSED: Yes, Your Worship

ACCUSED: Mr Kersop, how long have you been a traffic officer?

WITNESS: More than twenty-five years.

ACCUSED: You told this court that you traced and found me and also confirmed that it was the new commander. How would you expect me to know that you are a traffic officer? In you evidence in chief you testified you were not wearing traffic badges and you were, in fact, not identifiable as you had removed your jacket as it was too hot.

WITNESS: It is my duty to do that; my duty was to arrest you.

COURT: Mr Kersop, as a police officer, you have a legal duty to inform a person that you are a traffic officer and produce identification.

WITNESS: Everyone knew me in Cradock.

ACCUSED: I will leave that for argument because you are avoiding the answer.

ACCUSED: Mr Kersop, the Road Traffic Act and its regulations direct you to dress properly in that you must wear full uniform when you are on duty and, furthermore, must carry your appointment certificate at all times. If you were breaking the traffic laws, how do you expect an ordinary person like me to know that you are indeed a traffic officer?

WITNESS: People know me in Cradock.

ACCUSED: I am going to testify that I believed that I was defending myself from a stranger who was robbing my car. How do you respond to that?

WITNESS: I insist, I was on duty.

ACCUSED: In count 1, I am being charged for parking a vehicle in a disabled parking bay. I am going to testify that, on the day in question, I legally parked in the disabled parking because I was escorting Mr Lubabalo Ndingane, who was working in my office, and he could not walk properly because he was involved in an accident and that parking was the nearest to the chemist for him to get medication and he himself had to sign for his medical aid. How would you respond to that?

WITNESS: You should have told me.

ACCUSED: But you never introduce yourself. Do you still maintain that I committed any offence?

WITNESS: Yes.

ACCUSED: The Road Traffic Act directs you to record any incident in your diary or pocketbook. Can you furnish me with those records so that they can be read in this court?

WITNESS: I did not make records.

ACCUSED: But is your responsibility. How do expect this court to believe your testimony?

WITNESS: I am telling the truth.

ACCUSED: Where is the proof that you were, in fact, on duty?

WITNESS: I was on duty.

ACCUSED: Charge 2 is that I was driving a vehicle without a driver's licence. I put it to you that I do have a driver's licence and I was in possession of it on that day. I never saw a traffic officer; I saw a stranger and I was new in Cradock. Unless you were a traffic cop under cover, do you still believe that I drove the vehicle without a driver's licence?

COURT: You can respond to that question.

WITNESS: Yes. He did not produce it after I gave an instruction to do so.

ACCUSED: You are also running away from this question. Is there any commission of an offence, as I was in possession of the licence?

WITNESS: I disagree.

ACCUSED: Charge 3, is that I failed to furnish name and address as directed by a traffic officer. As I already put questions to you that indicate that I never saw a traffic officer – in fact, I saw a stranger – do you still maintain that I committed any offence?

WITNESS: Yes.

ACCUSED: I will deal with all these charges in my arguments.

ACCUSED: on Count 4, assault. Assault is defined as the intentional and unlawful cause of physical harm or injury to another. I put it to you that I saw a stranger robbing me and taking away my car, and I only grabbed you on your hands. Do the above elements qualify to be an assault?

WITNESS: Yes. You assaulted me.

ACCUSED: I am not going to waste the Court's time. I will reserve anything further for argument and I have no further questions, Your Worship.

COURT: Prosecutor, do you have any re-examination?

PROSECUTOR: No re-examination and I am closing my case.

COURT: Accused, you have a right to open your case and call witnesses if need be.

ACCUSED: Thank you, Your Worship. I am making an application for discharge in terms of Section 174 of the criminal procedure Act 1977, and it is my submission that on the available evidence presented before this court up to and until this stage, no reasonable court can find a person guilty and convict him. Your Worship, at this stage the Court is expected to consider the presented evidence by the state and make a finding whether this evidence will stand alone.

It comes to my mind the case of *S v Lubaxa (2001)(2)(sacr)* (SCA). The court made the following comments in dealing with a Section 174 application: "If, in opinion of the trial court, there is evidence upon which the accused might reasonably be convicted, the Court might not discharged the accused but, when the trial court is of the opinion that there is no evidence upon which the accused might be found not guilty, the Court must do so."

It is therefore against this background that I submit that there is no evidence presented by the state against me up to now that would convict me. Your Worship, my reasons are as follows: On COUNT 1 of parking a vehicle on a place marked for disabled persons, the State, through its sole witness, did not tender any evidence to the effect that they indeed investigated and confirmed whether I was indeed helping an injured person until the end of the State case.

With regard to COUNT 2, driving a motor vehicle without a driver's licence, a question was put to the witness whether he or an investigating officer came to me to check whether I indeed have a driver's licence, but no-one did that until today.

COUNT 3, failing to comply with instructions of a traffic officer. The so-called traffic officer testified that he had removed his jacket with badges and name tag. There is no way that any normal person will take or obey instructions from stranger, especially with this high crime rate in South Africa.

COUNT 4, assault. Assault is defined as the intentional and unlawful application of force to a person by another and, for an assault case to stand, there must be elements of crime and the attacker or person accused of assault must not have any grounds of justification. I want to draw a picture, Your Worship, where I was sitting in a car and stranger appeared and grabbed my car keys without any notice. In that scenario, I want to refer to Snyman and his book called *Criminal Law South Africa* and a section on grounds of justification. It says in his book: "for the accused to succeed in his defence of self-defence, it must be directed against the attacker and defender has injured the attacker while defending or protecting his or her legal interest and was no other way at that time except to injure the attacker."

For these reasons, Your Worship, I am applying for discharge.

COURT: What do you say, Prosecutor?

PROSECUTOR: I will leave to the Court to decide.

COURT: JUDGMENT

At this stage of the proceedings, the Court is called upon to decide whether or not at the close of the State case for the prosecution it is of the opinion that there is evidence that the accused committed an offence referred in the charges. Firstly, I must mention that I was not happy with the way that this case was handled from the beginning. The DPP's office instructed that certain charges be put to the accused and the State put other charges or more charges.

The only witness Mr Kersop, who was really an honest witness, simply tells the truth. For instance, if he did not follow procedure he simply agreed. He testified that, on the day in question, it was too hot and he decided to remove his jacket and thus did not appear as a traffic officer. It is clear that neither the investigating officer nor Mr Kersop ever informed the accused of his rights in terms of Section 35 of the Constitution and they have a legal duty to do. The quality of evidence presented by the State give a benefit of doubt in favour of the accused. The traffic officer never followed the procedures as directed by Traffic Regulations. Therefore, the accused will be given the benefit of doubt and is found not guilty.

ACCUSED: As the Court pleases

While I was found not guilty in court, I was already on the way to Grahamstown as I had been promoted to the rank of Lieutenant Colonel, but I was served with notice of suspension without pay and I was charged with thirty-six departmental charges.

I wrote several letters to the police management and police minister but the only response was that the matter would be investigated, but that never happened.

Notice of suspension.

Suid~Afrikaanse Polisiediens  South African Police Service

Private Bag　X 7471 King William's Town	**Fax**　043 604 6306 041 585 4116 086 515 3931

YOUR REFERENCE

MY REFERENCE　0490165-7/5

ENQUIRIES　Brigadier RH Botha

TEL.　043 604 6305
041 504 5698

THE PROVINCIAL HEAD

SOUTH AFRICAN POLICE SERVICE

CRIMINAL RECORD CENTRE

EASTERN CAPE

KING WILLIAM'S TOWN

2011-05-11

A The Cluster Commander
South African Police Service
GRAHAMSTOWN

Attention: Brig Moyake

B The Head
South African Police Service
Criminal Record and Crime Scene Management
PRETORIA

Attention: Maj Gen Khunou

ALLEGED MISCONDUCT: NOTICE OF INTENDED SUSPENSION: NO 0490165-7 LIEUTENANT COLONEL T MAQEBHULA: GRAHAMSTOWN LCRC

A1.　Appended herewith please find notice of intended suspension of Lt Col Maqebhula, as received from the office of the Provincial Commissioner.

2.　Kindly provide this office with a copy of the return of service, once an acknowledgement of receipt has been obtained

Kindly fax to 0865153931

Your cooperation would be appreciated

Copy for your good office's information

Kind regards

_____________　BRIGADIER
PROVINCIAL HEAD : CRC : EASTERN CAPE
BOTHA

CHAPTER FIVE

Letter from National Commissioners' office, dated 2010/07/19

South African Police Service   Suid-Afrikaanse Polisiediens

Private Bag Privaatsak	X98 Pretoria	Fax No: Faks No:	(012) 393-1631

Your reference/U verwysing:

My reference/My verwysing   0469858-0/5

Enquiries/Navrae: Major-General BC Mgwenya

Tel: (012) 393-1616/7

THE NATIONAL COMMISSIONER
DIE NASIONALE KOMMISSARIS

PRETORIA

0001

2010 -07- 1 9

Office of the Commander
LCRC
SA Police Service
GRAHAMSTOWN
6141

MAL-ADMINISTRATION OR DEFEATING THE ENDS OF JUSTICE : INVESTIGATION : DEPARTMENTAL HEARING : CASE NO. 45/12/2007 (FRAUD) PERSAL NUMBER (CRADOCK LCRC

By direction of the National Commissioner of the South African Police Service , we hereby acknowledge receipt of your letter with the concerns as indicated above.

The matter has been referred to Deputy National Commissioner : Personnel Management and Organisational Development for investigation, and you can expect feedback from her office. The contact details are :- (012) 393 2630 (Tel) and (012) 393 1033 (Fax).

Kind regards

MAJOR-GENERAL
OFFICE OF THE NATIONAL COMMISSIONER : SOUTH AFRICAN POLICE SERVICE
C MGWENYA

Letter from the Office of the Provincial Commissioner, Eastern Cape

SAPS 21

SUID-AFRIKAANSE POLISIEDIENS   **SOUTH AFRICAN POLICE SERVICE**

OFFICE OF THE PROVINCIAL COMMISSION!
SOUTH AFRICAN POLICE SERVICE
PROVINCIAL INSPECTORATE
PRIVATE BAG X7471
KING WILLIAM'S TOWN
EASTERN CAPE

Verwysing / Reference	4/14/2/1/8(4)
Navrae / Enquiries	Brig Teka
Telefoon / Telephone	(040) 608 7097 / (040) 608 7090
Faksnommer / Fax number	(040) 608 7122/095

A.   The Divisional Commissioner
     National Inspectorate
     South African Police Service
     Private Bag 94
     PRETORIA   **Att: Maj Gen Vuma**

B.   The Divisional Commissioner
     Criminal Record & Forensic Science Service
     South African Police Service
     PRETORIA   **Att: Lt Gen Pahlane**

C.   The Provincial Head
     Criminal & Record Centre
     Private Bag X 7471
     KING WILLAIMS TOWN   **Att: Brig Botha**

D.   The Commander
     Criminal Record and Crime Science Management
     South African Police Service
     GRAHAMSTOWN   **Att: Lt Col Maqebula**

ALLEGED INTERFERENCE BY BRIG BOTHA TO LCRC GRAHAMSTOWN: COMPLAINANT LT COL MAQEBULA

A   1.   Telephone conversation between Maj Gen Rapudi and Brig Teka on 2011/10/04 and my evenly numbered dated 2011/06/29 refers.

    2.   Both Brig Botha and Lt Col Maqebula keep on requesting feedback from this office on the complaint which was submitted to your office on 2011/06/29. Since then no response was received from your office.

B   1.   Copy for your information.

    2.   Addressee "B"'s letter dated 2011/08/22 which was also sent to your office bears reference on this matter.

C.   1.   Copy for your information.

      2.   Attached herewith is a copy of the letter received from addressee "D"
            for your information and communication with Maj Gen Vuma of
            National Inspectorate who according to Maj Gen Rapudi this matter
            was referred to her for handling.

D.   1.   Copy for your information.

                                        MAJ GENERAL
F/PROVINCIAL COMMISSIONER: EASTERN CAPE
E N DLANI
DATE:

34

Letter from the Provincial Commissioner, Eastern Cape, dated 2011/12/29

G.S -9. 002-0222

SUID-AFRIKAANSE POLISIEDIENS

SOUTH AFRICAN POLICE SERVICE

Verwysing Reference	4/14/2/1/8(4)
Navrae Enquiries	4/14/2/3(915) Brig. Teka
Telefoon Telephone	(040) 6087 097
Faksnommer Fax number	(040) 6087 095

OFFICE OF THE PROVINCIAL COMMISSIONER
SOUTH AFRICAN POLICE SERVICE
PROVINCIAL INSPECTORATE
PRIVATE BAG X7471
KINGWILLIAM'S TOWN
EASTERN CAPE

29 December 2011

A.   The Divisional Commissioner
South African Police Service
Private bag X 94
PRETORIA   Att : Maj Gen Vuma

B.   The Provincial Head
Criminal Record and Crime Management Centre
Private Bag X 7471
KING WILLIAMSTOWN   Att : Brig Botha

C.   The Commander
Local Criminal Record Centre
GRAHAMSTOWN   Att : Lieut Col Maqebula

D.   The Provincial Commissioner
South African Police Service
EASTERN CAPE

E.   The Provincial Manager
South African Human Rights Commission
P O Box 972
EAST LONDON   Att : Adv L Mpondo

ALLEGED INTERFERENCE BY BRIG BOTHA TO LCRC GRAHAMSTOWN ADMINISTRATION:

A.1.   The above mentioned complaint was forwarded to your office in June 2011 for your assistance.

2.   Seeing that no acknowledgement of receipt was received, a telephone call was made to Maj Gen Rapudi who referred the matter to Brig Nentswera. Brig Nentswera phoned Brig Teka and promised to come to the Eastern Cape to investigate the complaint. Since then, no communication between this office and your office was received and

the complaint is now over six (6) months without any investigation conducted.

3. The allegations against Brig Botha are regarded serious by both Brig Botha and Lieut Col Maqebula who is the complainant in this matter.

4. . The complaint was further sent to the office of the Human Rights Commission by the Complainant and that office is still waiting for a response from our office. ,

5. Head Office is hereby requested to indicate whether the investigation was conducted and what was the outcome thereof.

B-D.1 Copy for your information.

E.1. Copy for your information.

2. Your letter Ref.EC 2011/0260/NT dated 2011/09/06 refers.

MAJ GENERAL
PROVINCIAL HEAD: INSPECTORATE:EC
X C NTANTISO

Letter from the office of the Divisional Commissioner, dated 2012/01/12

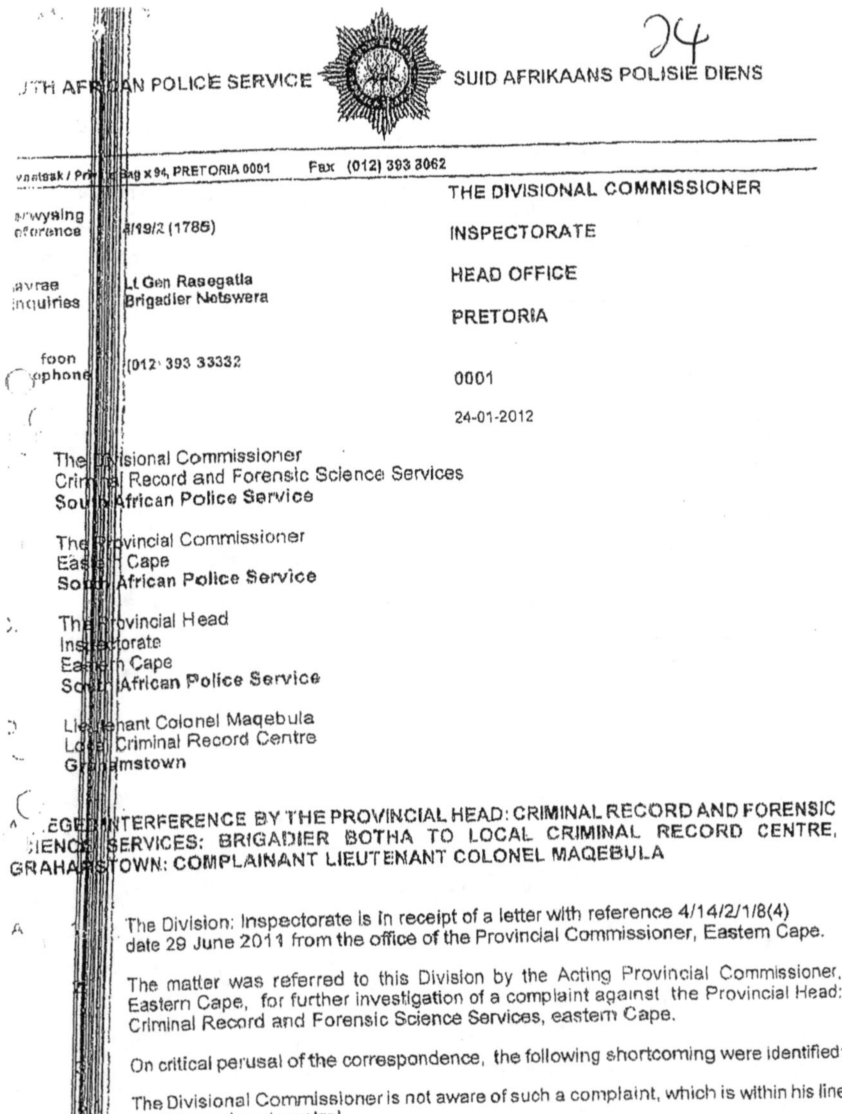

SOUTH AFRICAN POLICE SERVICE · SUID AFRIKAANS POLISIE DIENS

Verwysing / Private Bag X 94, PRETORIA 0001   Fax (012) 393 3062

aanwysing reference	4/19/2 (1785)

THE DIVISIONAL COMMISSIONER

INSPECTORATE

HEAD OFFICE

PRETORIA

navrae inquiries	Lt Gen Rasegatla Brigadier Netswera
foon telephone	(012) 393 33332

0001

24-01-2012

The Divisional Commissioner
Criminal Record and Forensic Science Services
South African Police Service

The Provincial Commissioner
Eastern Cape
South African Police Service

The Provincial Head
Inspectorate
Eastern Cape
South African Police Service

Lieutenant Colonel Maqebula
Local Criminal Record Centre
Grahamstown

ALLEGED INTERFERENCE BY THE PROVINCIAL HEAD: CRIMINAL RECORD AND FORENSIC SCIENCE SERVICES: BRIGADIER BOTHA TO LOCAL CRIMINAL RECORD CENTRE, GRAHAMSTOWN: COMPLAINANT LIEUTENANT COLONEL MAQEBULA

The Division: Inspectorate is in receipt of a letter with reference 4/14/2/1/8(4) date 29 June 2011 from the office of the Provincial Commissioner, Eastern Cape.

The matter was referred to this Division by the Acting Provincial Commissioner, Eastern Cape, for further investigation of a complaint against the Provincial Head: Criminal Record and Forensic Science Services, eastern Cape.

On critical perusal of the correspondence, the following shortcoming were identified:

The Divisional Commissioner is not aware of such a complaint, which is within his line of command and control.

This matter was sent from pillar to post, which subsequently delayed the attention it deserves.

3.3   The seriousness of this matter requires a senior officer to address it because it borders the management of the office.

4.   The above mentioned information suggests that the matter should be referred to your Division for attention.

5.   However, if you decide that the Division: Inspectorate should investigate it, then this office will address the matter.

B-D   1.   For your information.

Kind Regards

....MAJOR GENERAL
F/ DIVISIONAL COMMISSIONER: INSPECTORATE
SOUTH AFRICAN POLICE SERVICE
SC RAPHUTI
Date   2012 -01- 2 4

MINISTRY OF POLICE
REPUBLIC OF SOUTH AFRICA

Private Bag X463 PRETORIA 0001, Tel: (012) 393 2800, Fax: (012) 393 2819/20 • Private Bag X9080 CAPE TOWN 8000, Tel: (021) 467 7021, Fax: (021) 467 7033

REFERENCE: **3/1/4/1/5(17/2009)**

Lt T Maqebhula
Criminal Records & Crime Scene Management
Private Bag x 1
Eastern Cape
GRAHAMSTOWN

Fax: 046 6039327

Dear Lt Maqebhula

ALLEGED RASCIM, COVERS-UP AND FAILURE BY SAPS MANAGEMENT TO ADDRESS COMPLAINTS: LCRC

On behalf of the Minister of Police, Mr EN Mthethwa, MP, we hereby acknowledge receipt of your correspondence dated 12th April 2013.

Kindly be informed that the matter has been referred to the National Commissioner of South African Police Services for further attention.

You may therefore expect further correspondence from his office in due course.

With kind regards.

AMELIAH MASHEGO
ADMINISTRATIVE SECRETARY
DATE: 23 APR 2013

CHAPTER SIX

Departmental Trial

THE SUSPENSION WAS UNSUCCESSFUL BECAUSE I also took the matter too high to interdict, but I was finally charged departmentally, as case no 51/04 /2011.

From day one of the trial, I represented myself and raised points in limine on a number of issues such as procedural fairness and the use of illegally obtained evidence in violation of my constitutional rights, particularly Section 35 of the Constitution, 1996.

My argument was as follows: In December 2010, I opened up a case of the theft of official documents from my office. It was registered as Grahamstown case 329/12/2010 and at that time there was no suspect.

But, when I was charged departmentally, a police colonel, purporting to be the investigating officer, came to my office for the first time and informed me that he had been appointed to investigate me departmentally and handed all documentation to me.

When I perused the documents, I noticed that copies of those stolen documents were filed as evidence against me. The first point in limine was:

(A) Procedural Fairness, in that I was never been informed of any departmental investigation in contravention of South African Police Disciplinary Regulation, read with Schedule 8 of the Labour Relations Act, 1995. This says that says that, if the employer or supervisor suspects misconduct by his employee, she or he must start investigations or appoint a person to do so, and in the process the employee must be called upon and informed of the intended investigation, and must be given a chance to respond. The regulation in question also provides forms where the employee and employer must confirm that they were indeed informed. Disciplinary Regulations prescribe that the employer must appoint an investigator to deal with the case, but I noticed from the documents furnished to me that there were three investigating officers appointed to investigate the same disciplinary case and none of them ever informed me.

(B) Illegally obtained evidence in violation of Section 35(5) of the Constitution that says: evidence obtained in a manner that violates any right in the Bill of Rights must be excluded if the admission of that evidence would render the trial unfair or otherwise be detrimental to the administration of justice. At the trial, a colonel gave evidence to the effect that he got those copies of stolen documents from a brigadier, who was the complainant and my commander.

On the other hand, I had written a detailed letter to the investigating officer of the criminal case about the theft of stolen documents, informing him that I had the suspects of the case and the witnesses would be two colonels and they confirmed under oath that they had got the copies of stolen documents from that brigadier, my provincial head who was working at King Williams Town, although the documents had been stolen in Grahamstown. Having not got assistance from the branch detective commander, I took the matter to the office of the provincial commissioner, Eastern Cape, but could not get help.

The departmental trial continued as the presiding officer ruled the case must proceed as the South African Police regulations make no provision for dismissal of a case if points in limine raised are allowed. He further said that he would consider them at the end of the trial.

After a long trial, I was found not guilty.

While still celebrating the not guilty verdict departmentally, I got a surprise summons from a Grahamstown detective, informing me that the Grahamstown Deputy Director of Public Prosecutions had decided to charge me for fraud, and I was given a prosecutorial note.

National Prosecution Service
Director of Public Prosecutions:
Grahamstown

National Prosecuting Authority of South Africa
Igunya Jikelele Labetshutshisi boMzantsi Afrika
Die Nasionale Vervolgingsgesag van Suid Afrika

EASTERN CAPE
HIGH COURT

Grahamstown

Tel: +27 46 602 3000
Fax: +27 46 602 3061
     +27 46 602 3062

94 High Street
GRAHAMSTOWN
6139

Private Bag X1009
GRAHAMSTOWN
6140
SOUTH AFRICA

www.npa.gov.za

Ref: P35/10
Enq: Adv. Mtsila
Date: 11 November 2010

The Senior Public Prosecutor
Private Bag X 1004
GRAHAMSTOWN
6140

THE STATE VERSUS TENGIMPILO MAQEBHULA
GRAHAMSTOWN CAS 648/02/2010

1. I have decided to arraign Tengimpilo Maqebhula at a summary trial before the Magistrate's Court on a charge of fraud.

2. I enclose a draft charge sheet.

3. The case docket, Grahamstown CAS 648/02/2010, is enclosed.

4. Please inform me of the outcome of the matter no later than 30 July 2011.

DIRECTOR OF PUBLIC PROSECUTIONS: GRAHAMSTOWN
MM

CHAPTER SEVEN

Incidents towards my next criminal case

I QUESTIONED THE DETECTIVE TO find out who the complainant of this case was, and where the case had been opened, but could not get an answer and I had more questions than answers. As I used be an investigating officer myself, I knew that, when you are tasked to investigate a criminal case, you first do the investigation. Once finished, you approach or arrest the person and inform that person of his rights in terms of Section 35(3) of the Constitution. The suspect is supposed to sign the warning statement, but this never happened to me.

I requested the copies of the dockets as per the Constitutional Court ruling in the case of *Tshabalala and Others v Attorney General of Transvaal* as well as Section 35(3) of the Constitution, 1996. When I was finished with the copies of the docket, I noticed that some copies of the stolen documents for Grahamstown cas 329/12/2010 were filed there as evidence against me.

I also noticed that there was no fraud case opened or reported anywhere in Grahamstown police stations. Surprisingly, I discovered that the reckless and negligent driving case, cas 648/02/2010, that I had been involved in and in which prosecution was declined, was quoted as the case number for the fraud case. Furthermore, I got correspondence addressed to my then lawyers advising that, if I wanted to plea bargain, I must consult an advocate from the Grahamstown DPP's office.

Letter dated 2011/02 inviting me to go for plea bargaining

SOUTH AFRICAN POLICE SERVICE   **3**   **SUID-AFRIKAANSE POLISIEDIENS**

My reference / My verwysing	CAS 648/02/2010
Enquiries / Navrae	W/O Lensley
Tel	046-6039111
E-mail	
Fax / Faks	046-6039304

OFFICE OF THE BRANCH COMMANDER
KANTOOR VAN DIE TAKBEVELVOERDER
DETECTIVE SERVICE / SPEURDIENS
PRIVATE BAG / PRIVAATSAK X1
MARKET SQUARE / MARKPLEIN
EASTERN CAPE / OOS-KAAP
GRAHAMSTOWN / GRAHAMSTAD
6140

28 February 2011

A   Hutton & Cook   Att Max
       King Williamstown   Fax no 043 - 6425581

**ALLEGED OFFENCE : NUMBER: 0490165-7: , RANK: LT COLONEL
NAME: T MAQEBHULA : GRAHAMSTOWN CAS 648/02/2010
(OFFENCE) RECKLESS & NEGLIGENT DRIVING/FRAUD**

1.   Attached find the J175, that was served on your client.

2   The court date is 2011/03/23

3   If you wish to enter in a Plea Bargaining agreement , you can contact Mr G Turner of the Director of Prosecutions office at Grahamstown

Colonel

L . Ngubelanga   COLONEL
BRANCH COMMANDER : DETECTIVE BRANCH
(L NGUBELANGA)   : GRAHAMSTOWN

Funny things happened. My then lawyers advised me to plead guilty and I also noticed that there was communication behind my back between my lawyers and the investigating officer. I decided to terminate my instructions to those lawyers.

Furthermore, the case was supposed to start with a certain magistrate but for some reason that magistrate was not available on that day, and another magistrate was appointed.

More funny things happened, in that the investigating officer who gave me summons to appear in the criminal trail came to my office and informed me that he had been sent by the prosecutor and told not to accept the date of the new magistrate who was going to deal with my case. I chased him away from my office.

Nevertheless the trial proceeded in Grahamstown District Court.

I released a statement in Grocotts Newspaper, dated 2011/05/2011, appealing to the community and police management for help.

NEWS

Grocott's Mail Tuesday, 24 May 2011

aud case against me a cover-up
ys top cop

KA

ior local policeman has
de the explosive claim that
ud charges against him
ressly intended to under-
objection to the fact that
with a criminal record was
in a crucial position at the
town police station.

el Tengimpilo Maqebhula
briefly in the Graham-
agistrate's Court on Tues-
ud charges.

ha ___ sheet alleges that on
ury 2010, Maqebhula signed
lice vehicle to drive from
town to Port Elizabeth for
poses.

ver, later that day, the car
lved in an accident not on
ut instead on the R350 be-
ahamstown and Bedford.

harge sheet further alleges
ebhula reported he had hit
1 his way to Port Elizabeth.
st, Maqebhula faced inter-
ges of "statutory reckless
gent driving".

n investigation, however,
the Fiat Siena he had been
unimal intestines and blood
ere found on the R350 three
er, and a fraud case was
gainst him.

ebhula now believes he has
gete a result of questions
een asking about the Crimi-
rd Centre since he was ap-

pointed its commander in 2009.

Promoted from the Cradock
Criminal Record Centre in 2009,
Maqebhula told *Grocott's Mail* that
when he arrived at the Grahamstown office he discovered that one
of the employees in his centre had a
criminal record that included theft,
forgery and fraud.

These crimes had not been reported to the South African Police
Service Criminal Bureau, however,
and this was contrary to the provisions of the Criminal Procedure Act
of 1977, which stated that "every ac-

cused person who is found guilty of
crime by a court of law should be
recorded with South African Police
Service Criminal Bureau".

Maqebhula said he had reported
the matter to the provincial Criminal
Record Centre management, telling
them that in terms of Criminal Bureau Ethics, the department could
not retain someone convicted of a
crime. They brushed him off, he said,
accusing him of being "too personal". Adding to his suspicion of some
kind of conspiracy, Maqebhula said,
was the fact that when he obtained

copies of the docket pertaining to his
fraud charge, he discovered that the
employee with the criminal record
was a witness in the case, along with
five other officers.

The matter was postponed to 12
July for plea and trial. Magistrate
Nishani Beharie said there were
other serious cases that day and
Maqebhula's case needed "too much
attention and time".

*Odwa Funeka is an independent
citizen journalist for* **Grocott's
Mail**

TOP COP IN THE DOCK... Local top cop Colonel Tengimpilo Maqebhula (left), chats with his legal representative Advocate Vuyani Msindo ahead of his fraud case which was postponed at the Grahamstown Magistrate's Court last week. Photo: Odwa Funeka

CHAPTER EIGHT

IN GRAHAMSTOWN:
IN THE MAGISTRATE'S COURT FOR THE EASTERN CAPE REGION HELD
AT: GRAHAMSTOWN
CASE NO C262/2011
DATE 12 JULY 2011
IN THE MATTER OF
STATE
VERSUS
T. MAQEBHULA: ACCUSED

PROSECUTOR: Accused is represented by a defence lawyer and the State is ready to proceed.

COURT: All witnesses are present?

PROSECUTOR: Yes.

DEFENCE LAWYER: May I confirm my appearance for the accused before court and we are ready.

COURT: You can proceed to put the matter on record.

PROSECUTOR: Case no C262/2011, State versus Tengimpilo Maqebhula. Today's date is the 12th of July 2011. The accused is guilty of fraud. The accused holds the rank of colonel in the SA Police Service. The accused is stationed at Grahamstown Local Criminal Record Centre, SAPS. The accused was driving a state vehicle from Port Elizabeth to Grahamstown. While on the way, he was involved in an accident in which he knocked down a kudu, and the vehicle was badly damaged. On further investigation by

Warrant Officer Lesley, it transpired that the accident took place near Bedford. The investigating officer Warrant Officer Lesley, who was initially tasked to investigate a reckless and negligent case, did not believe that the accident happened on the N2, as reported. He was of the view that the accident happened between Bedford and Grahamstown and therefore the accused committed fraud.

COURT: You understand the charges, Sir? I can just give you the charge sheet.

ACCUSED: Yes, I understand the charge

COURT: You want them to be interpreted?

COURT: How do you plead to charges?

ACCUSED: Pleads not guilty

COURT: Give him the charge

DEFENCE LAWYER: Your worship, the plea is in accordance with my instructions. I am further instructed to reserve the plea explanation at this stage.

COURT: You may be seated and state will proceed.

EVIDENCE ON BEHALF OF THE STATE
FIRST WITNESS: Mervin Wayne Frans
EXAMINATION BY PROSECUTOR

PROSECUTOR: Sir, you work for the South African Police Service and are stationed in Grahamstown, and you are a constable. Is that correct?

WITNESS: Yes, that is correct.

PROSECUTOR: To which unit are you attached?

WITNESS: High Patrol Unit in Grahamstown.

PROSECUTOR: Were you on duty on the 26th of February 2010?

WITNESS: Yes, I was on duty.

PROSECUTOR: What were some of your duties on that evening?

WITNESS: My duties involved patrolling the N2, attending to accident scenes, stopping and searching vehicles and roadblocks.

PROSECUTOR: Sir, you responded to an accident that day.

WITNESS: Yes. I got a call on the radio from control room Grahamstown Police Station, informing me about the accident and I was instructed to go and investigate.

PROSECUTOR: What happened during your investigation?

WITNESS: The vehicle was already at VISS and on my arrival the driver, Colonel Maqebhula, came to me and explained what happened, in that he was involved in an accident in a state vehicle, a Fiat Siena. He said he had knocked a kudu as he was driving towards Grahamstown from Port Elizabeth

Then I notified Colonel Soldaat, who was the shift commander, and we went together with the Colonel and visited the scene on the N2 and Colonel Maqebhula pointed out the scene.

PROSECUTOR: You were then shown the scene of the accident and what happened.

WITNESS: I then opened a case of reckless and negligent driving, as it is the procedure when a state vehicle is involved and the case was registered as Grahamstown cas 646/02/2010 and the charge was reckless and negligent driving.

PROSECUTOR: Now you say you opened a case and what happened?

COURT: So you left the vehicle where it was, and notified the standby duty officer?

PROSECUTOR: This is the procedure to be followed when state vehicles are involved.

WITNESS: Yes. But if there is a high flow of vehicles and it is a busy day like a Friday, and if no person is injured, we normally remove vehicles from crime scenes and mark all points and attend on the next day that is not busy. So this is what happened to Colonel Maqebhula, as no person was injured.

PROSECUTOR: How long were you working at SAPS?

WITNESS: Five years.

NO FURTHER QUESTIONS BY PROSECUTOR

CROSS EXAMINATION BY LAWYER

DEFENCE LAWYER: As the court pleases, Your Worship, Mr Frans, what is the rank that you are holding currently?

WITNESS: I am a constable.

DEFENCE LAWYER: Now, I am interested to know: When you got to the scene of the accident, you told this court that yourself, the accused and Colonel Soldaat went to the scene of accident?

WITNESS: We went on the N2, twenty kilometres to Grahamstown

DEFENCE LAWYER: And you further told the Court that at the scene of the accident, the accused pointed out the scene where the collision took place. Is that correct?

WITNESS: Yes, that it is correct.

DEFENCE LAWYER: So he pointed out a mark, indicating the place where the accident took place.

WITNESS: Yes, and there were small pieces of meat and glass lying on the road.

DEFENCE LAWYER: After Colonel Maqebhula pointed out everything, were you satisfied with the explanation?

WITNESS: Yes, I was satisfied.

DEFENCE LAWYER: Was the explanation given by Colonel Maqebhula consistent with the damage to vehicle?

WITNESS: Yes it was, and I was satisfied.

DEFENCE LAWYER: All you know is what you observed on the 26th of February 2010?

WITNESS: Yes.

DEFENCE LAWYER: And I am asking you exactly about that. From what you observed, can you tell the Court with certainty that, according to you, the collision took place exactly where the accused pointed it out to you?

WITNESS: Yes.

DEFENCE LAWYER: So, the summary of your evidence is that there was nothing wrong with what you observed on the day against the accused?

WITNESS: Yes.

NO FURTHER QUESTIONS

Evidence of Warrant Officer Lesley as investigating officer, pointing officer and a witness

EVIDENCE ON BEHALF OF THE STATE
BAREND DANIEL LESLEY
EXAMINATION BY PROSECUTOR

PROSECUTOR: Sir, you are employed by the South African Police Services and you are stationed at Grahamstown Police Station. Is that correct?

WITNESS: That is correct, Your Worship.

PROSECUTOR: Now, how long have you been working for the South African Police Services?

WITNESS: Your Worship, I have got seventeen years' service in the police.

PROSECUTOR: And to which unit are you attached?

WITNESS: Currently, I am attached to the CID Branch, the detective branch, Your Worship.

PROSECUTOR: And to which unit were you attached in February in 2010?

PROSECUTOR: I was attached to the Detectives, Your Worship.

PROSECUTOR: Now, Sir, you are also the investigating officer in the case which is before court today. Is that correct?

WITNESS: That is correct, Your Worship.

PROSECUTOR: Now, have you conducted investigations regarding the case which is before the Court today?

WITNESS: Yes, Your Worship.

PROSECUTOR: Can you tell the Court what happened regarding the incident of the 26th of February 2010?

WITNESS: Your Worship, I received a docket on the Monday after the incident happened.

PROSECUTOR: When did the incident occur?

WITNESS: It happened on the Friday, Your Worship, the precise date I am not a hundred percent sure, Your Worship.

PROSECUTOR: Proceed. You received a docket and what happened?

WITNESS: Your Worship, then I was investigating cases against members of the South African Police Services. At that stage, Your Worship, I was informed and I got information that the accident where it is alleged to have happened on the N2 did not happen there. It is alleged that it happened on the Bedford Road, Your Worship. I then requested Warrant Officer Van Onselon to go and show me the place of the accident

PROSECUTOR: Slow down, Sir, please.

WITNESS: Okay, sorry.

PROSECUTOR: You say that you received the information about the accident which occurred on the Bedford Road.

WITNESS: It was alleged that the accident happened according to the case docket on the N2 towards Port Elizabeth, but the information I received was it did not happen there, it happened on the road from Grahamstown towards Bedford, Your Worship

PROSECUTOR: Okay, and after you received this information, what happened?

WITNESS: Your Worship, I then requested Warrant Officer van Onselen, who was the member of LCRC on standby, to go and show me the incident that was pointed out to him on the N2, how it looks like there, so I could know what the situation was there. He then took me to a pass – it is about twenty or twenty-five kilometres out on N2 – and he showed me where the incident allegedly happened, Your Worship.

PROSECUTOR: Proceed.

WITNESS: Your Worship, on the scene there I noticed a piece of blood, or it looked like blood to me. It was about the diameter say of about a small saucepan, and I was not convinced.

PROSECUTOR: Sir, what made you to come to that conclusion?

WITNESS: Your Worship, the amount of blood and the amount of debris that was there was not much.

PROSECUTOR: Proceed. What happened thereafter?

WITNESS: I then went back to the office and I requested Warrant Officer de Klerk, who is a photographer, to go with me and then I went out on the Bedford Road to look for the accident.

PROSECUTOR: Can I just ask, where did you get the information that the accident had occurred in the Bedford road?

WITNESS: Your Worship, it was from a source I don't want to reveal.

COURT: Okay, fine. If you don't want to disclose your source that is fine, but then it cannot be admissible in court.

PROSECUTOR: And then you asked Warrant officer De Klerk to accompany you towards the Bedford road?

WITNESS: That is correct.

PROSECUTOR: What did you do with regard to exhibits from the N2 road scene?

WITNESS: Your Worship, I just picked up those pieces of debris that were there and I took them to my office, Your Worship, and took the blood that I saw there, alleged blood, and I put in a security bag and sealed it, Your Worship, and then later that debris I handed into the SAP 13, Your Worship.

PROSECUTOR: Are you referring to the pieces and blood which you saw on the N2?

WITNESS: Yes.

PROSECUTOR: So you placed them into the bag and thereafter what did your do with them?

WITNESS: I went to my office, Your Worship, and I put it in my office and locked it in the safe.

COURT: That is the blood as well?

WITNESS: The blood as well, Your Worship.

PROSECUTOR: In what form was this blood? Was it liquid?

WITNESS: Dry. It was dry.

PROSECUTOR: You are referring to pieces of debris, if I am correct?

WITNESS: That is correct, Your Worship.

PROSECUTOR: What were these pieces of blood. What did they look like?

WITNESS: It was a big piece of blood. I remember clearly another one is a big piece of plastic.

COURT: Is it part of a vehicle?

WITNESS: Yes, Your Worship

PROSECUTOR: You say it was similar to a piece that was missing there?

WITNESS: Yes.

PROSECUTOR: Can you dwell on that one? Similar to a piece that was missing there; what do you mean?

WITNESS: Your Worship, after I went to the Bedford Road and I found the scene and everything, the next day I went to the motor vehicle itself that was involved in the accident, Your Worship. Obviously, I did some observation and I took blood from there as well and then, if you are sitting in the driver's seat, Your Worship, and it is my observation – I am not an expert regarding that – it is just what…

PROSECUTOR: You thereafter asked another person, Warrant Officer de Klerk, is that correct?

WITNESS: That is correct, Your Worship. I requested him to go with me and then we can see if he can gets this alleged accident scene on the Bedford road, Your Worship.

PROSECUTOR: Now, where did you go with him, or did he accompany you?

WITNESS: He got into my vehicle, Your Worship.

PROSECUTOR: And where did you go with him?

WITNESS: Your worship, we then drove on the Bedford Road – I wasn't sure how far this was – and we drove and drove and then about, I estimated about, twenty kilometres from Bedford – I know the turn off there says Malanskraal – there I saw a huge piece of blood and there you could see, it is a place where an accident took place with an animal. And I collected all exhibits and I then sealed all these exhibits that I picked up in forensic bags and also took samples of what looked like blood to me there.

Warrant officer de Klerk took photos of the Bedford scene. And then on the next day I went out to the motor vehicle that was parked at the VIS Unit in Grahamstown. Then I looked and I made my observations.

Then a couple of days later, I took a mechanic, Mr Goliath, to go with me and on his arrival he cut off a piece of that bumper that I pointed out in photo 44 and 45, Your Worship. I then sealed that in a security bag and placed both the two security evidence bags in a bigger bag and it was handed over to Sergeant Oosthuizen to take down to the lab in Port Elizabeth, Your Worship.

PROSECUTOR: You took the sample to the lab?

WITNESS: Well, Mr Oosthuizen took them to the lab. The plastic pieces he took down to the lab, Your Worship.

PROSECUTOR: And what happened thereafter?

WITNESS: Blood, or I presume blood, was also sent away, but unfortunately DNA could not be done on kudu blood. There is no result regarding that, Your Worship.

PROSECUTOR: What did this blood look like? Was it fresh or was it an old mark?

WITNESS: No, Your Worship, it was okay. I won't be able to say how old it is but it was very dry; it is not recently over the weekend that a vehicle would have been involved in an accident there, Your Worship. There were no maggots and stuff like that, saying that it was very old, Your Worship.

PROSECUTOR: Now I notice here on pictures, photo 26 to photo 29, or photo 28, that the colour of the photos are blue, the colour of the objects that you picked up actually?

WITNESS: Your Worship, it actually looks more, it is more silver. It is a silver piece of, I presume, I am not an expert, Your Worship, but I presume it is probably a light behind the light or something but I am not an expert to say why it is like that.

NO FURTHER QUESTIONS BY PROSECUTOR

CROSS-EXAMINATION

DEFENCE LAWYER: Mr Lesley, are you Warrant Officer Lesley?

WITNESS: That is correct, Your Worship.

DEFENCE LAWYER: For how long have you been a police officer?

WITNESS: Your Worship, seventeen years, Your Worship.

DEFENCE LAWYER: And how long have you been an investigating officer?

WITNESS: I have been 14 years the investigating officer, Your Worship.

DEFENCE LAWYER: In relation to the 26th of February, for how long had you been an investigating officer in 2010?

WITNESS: About 13 years with investigation experience, Your Worship.

DEFENCE LAWYER: So you are an experienced investigator?

WITNESS: Your Worship, I have been an investigating officer. I won't say I am experienced, but I have done investigations.

DEFENCE LAWYER: Okay. You advised the Court that you received a docket of the reckless and negligent driving case on a Monday following the Friday of the collision?

WITNESS: That is correct, Your Worship.

DEFENCE LAWYER: Okay, and you were then tasked to investigate the case of reckless and negligent driving?

WITNESS: That is correct, Your Worship.

DEFENCE LAWYER: Then what did you do with the docket on the Monday?

WITNESS: Your Worship, I am not a hundred percent sure, but I received the docket, it was given to me, and I started with my investigation, Your Worship.

DEFENCE LAWYER: I am interested in what you did as your first step of investigation upon receiving the docket?

WITNESS: Your Worship, I said I went out to the scene on the N2 road to see what the situation was there

DEFENCE LAWYER: With whom did you go to the N2 road?

WITNESS: Warrant Officer van Onselen.

DEFENCE LAWYER: Was that on Monday, when you received the docket?

WITNESS: That is correct, Your Worship

DEFENCE LAWYER: Okay. Back from the N2 with Warrant Officer van Onselen, what did you do?

WITNESS: I took the exhibits that I got there to my office and then requested Warrant Officer de Klerk to go with me onto the Bedford road.

DEFENCE LAWYER: Come on. The accident happened on the 26th of February 2010. On the 1st of March, Monday morning, you received the docket and information at the same time?

WITNESS: That is correct, Your Worship.

DEFENCE LAWYER: Does it mean that on the very same Monday you received the information that the collision might have taken place somewhere else other than the N2?

WITNESS: That is correct, Your Worship.

DEFENCE LAWYER: And that was before you proceeded to the N2 scene of collision?

WITNESS: That is correct, Your Worship

DEFENCE LAWYER: Okay. From whom did you receive the information?

WITNESS: Your Worship, I don't want to disclose the person's name

DEFENCE LAWYER: Do you realise that the source of this information is very important in this case?

WITNESS: Your Worship, I don't see why. It was information that I followed up. If there had been no accident on the Bedford road, I would have come back and that would have been the end of it.

DEFENCE LAWYER: No, but that in not my question, Mr Lesley. Do you realise the importance of us knowing the source of the information that has led us to be here today?

WITNESS: Your Worship, like I said, I am not a hundred percent sure what is being asked.

DEFENCE LAWYER: Okay. Now, at what stage did you for the first time give the docket to the Public Prosecutor?

WITNESS: Your Worship, I'd have to go and look in the docket for when it was sent in for decision, Your Worship, but it was a couple of months.

DEFENCE LAWYER: Okay. Now, after the couple of months that you are referring to, when sending the docket to the Public Prosecutor what was the charge that was there in the docket and what was the charge against the accused?

WITNESS: Your Worship, he was informed and warned in respect of a case of reckless and negligent driving and he did give me a statement and it was attached to his warning statement after I warned him according to his rights, Your Worship.

DEFENCE LAWYER: You are then telling the Court that, after a couple of months when the docket was given to the Public Prosecutor, the accused had been warned of the reckless and negligent driving charge. Is that what you are saying?

WITNESS: That is correct, Your Worship.

DEFENCE LAWYER: I am trying to understand you well, Warrant Officer. In your evidence in chief, you testified that you received the docket on Monday the 1st and you also received the information on Monday, the same day. Is that correct?

WITNESS: Correct, your worship.

DEFENCE LAWYER: On the 3rd of March 2010, you had already visited all scenes, but you still warned the accused in respect of N2 scene.

WITNESS: Yes, I warned the accused in respect of the collision which took place.

DEFENCE LAWYER: Okay, are you then telling the Court that, although by then you had information and had investigated such information, but when the docket was brought to the Public Prosecutor the accused had been warned of a reckless and negligent driving charge that took place on the N2 road?

WITNESS: Your Worship, the time I took the warning statement from the accused, Your Worship, the information or the evidence that I had in my possession was that of an accident that happened on the N2.

DEFENCE LAWYER: It is your testimony that you received the docket and the information on the 1st of March and, according the warning statement, your took his statement on the 3rd.

COURT: Sorry, if I understand your question, you are saying that after the docket was submitted for decision a warning statement was given to him for neck and neck. Is that what you are saying?

DEFENCE LAWYER: What I am saying, Your Worship, is as at the time the docket was brought to the Public Prosecutor the accused had been warned of reckless and negligent driving.

COURT: Yes. Was that before or after it was given to the Prosecutor? I don't understand what your question is.

DEFENCE LAWYER: At the time the docket was being brought to the Prosecutor.

COURT: So before or after it was brought?

DEFENCE LAWYER: Before.

COURT: Yes. Please make that clear, because otherwise I become vague.

DEFENCE LAWYER: As the Court pleases, let me just rephrase the question. Warrant Officer Lesley, as at the Monday following the day of the collision on the 26th of February, you had known and you had information that the collision did not take place on the N2 as alleged by the accused.

WITNESS: Your Worship, I had information but I didn't have evidence, Your Worship.

DEFENCE LAWYER: Okay, and you had evidence even to the extent of photos being taken on the Bedford road as at that time?

WITNESS: That is correct, Your Worship.

DEFENCE LAWYER: Yes. Now, after a couple of months when you were taking the docket to the Public Prosecutor, you had warned the accused in respect of a collision that took place on the N2 road?

WITNESS: Your Worship, if I can explain in this way. When I get a docket and I investigate a docket I do all the investigation that is available. I finish with the warning statement. I can have a look at a docket and I can say precisely the date I took it and precisely the date the docket went to the Prosecutor. At the stage I took the warning statement, I did not have evidence to say that this man had an accident on the Bedford road. Your Worship, that is why I took his statement regarding the accident on the N2 and then I waited for the Prosecutor's decision to say on what charges he will be charged and then the way forward is from there, Your Worship.

DEFENCE LAWYER: Okay. In other words, you decided to conceal the information and let the Public Prosecutor decide on what allegedly took place on the N2 road until you received further information?

WITNESS: Your Worship, I did not conceal the evidence. I handed the docket over to the Prosecutor with the intention that they must make a decision and put the charges that may be put there, Your Worship.

DEFENCE LAWYER: Okay, now did, if you still recall, the Public Prosecutor make a decision?

WITNESS: Your Worship, the Public Prosecutor, yes, I remember correctly, did make a decision and requested us to forward the docket to the director of Public Prosecutions for his decision.

DEFENCE LAWYER: I want you to understand the question and be very careful of your answer on this. Don't dwell on it very much because I am not going to allow you to change your answer later on. Let me repeat the question, if you still recall. Take your time and think about it. Did the Public Prosecutor make a decision on the reckless and negligent driving charge in respect on the N2 collision?

WITNESS: This is correct.

DEFENCE LAWYER: Okay, that is exactly the reason I said you must take your time with this. It is very important. You have just given evidence to the Court to say that the Public Prosecutor gave a decision that you must take the docket to the DPP for that decision

WITNESS: That is correct, Your Worship.

DEFENCE LAWYER: Let me repeat my question. You told the Court that the decision of the Public Prosecutor was that you must take the docket to the DPP for a further decision. Is that what you said?

WITNESS: That is correct, Your Worship.

DEFENCE LAWYER: Okay, and it is after I warned you of the importance of this piece of evidence. You then requested the docket and when the docket is before you, you the tell the Court now that this is not the original; the original got lost?

WITNESS: That is correct, Your Worship.

DEFENCE LAWYER: I must warn you for the second time that this is very important. Don't move us around here.

COURT: You will get what my point is. You are now telling the Court that the decision of the Public Prosecutor was there is no case that can be made for reckless and negligent driving.

WITNESS: If I remember correctly, yes, Your Worship.

DEFENCE LAWYER: Okay, so what you are telling the Court about taking it back was not correct?

WITNESS: I don't take it back?

DEFENCE LAWYER: What you are telling the Court is that the Public Prosecutor said you must take the docket back to the DPP was not correct?

WITNESS: If I remember correctly, Your Worship, I said the docket must go to the DPP. I didn't say it must go back.

DEFENCE LAWYER: Now you further tell the Court that the Public Prosecutor advised you that the only case that can be made if properly investigated is the one of defeating the ends of justice?

WITNESS: If I remember correctly, yes. Your Worship, it was something to that effect.

DEFENCE LAWYER: Okay, and you don't recall the instructions of the Public Prosecutor?

WITNESS: I cannot a hundred percent remember each word, Your Worship.

DEFENCE LAWYER: And a directive was given to you as to what must then be investigated towards the case of defeating the ends of justice?

WITNESS: Your Worship, I remember there was something written about defeating the ends of justice, but also that the docket must then be taken to the DPP, Your Worship. There could have been other instructions, but I can't precisely remember each instruction, Your Worship.

DEFENCE LAWYER: Okay. It is correct that the accused managed to request and obtain the copies of the docket as at that time, and with me I have a copy of C6, where the entries of the Public Prosecutor were made as to what must be done in that case. Now, from the copy that I have, it is clearly written by the Public Prosecutor that there is a possibility of prosecution for defeating of ends of justice, and this is very important so listen to it: in that regard, please comply with the following. A12 and A13 must be amended to defeating the ends of justice not reck and neck (2) how did the vehicle get to VIS (3) a copy of the trip authority. And then at the bottom, the Public Prosecutor appended his or her signature. I have now reminded you. Wasn't that an instruction from the Public Prosecutor to you?

COURT: Yes, then you can ask the question.

DEFENCE LAWYER: As the Court pleases. My question is that, now I have reminded you, wasn't that an instruction to you by the Public Prosecutor?

WITNESS: Worship, if that is what is written on the copy, I can't dispute it. Unfortunately, the original docket went missing so I can't confirm with the original docket to say if it was there or not, Your Worship.

COURT: Do you recall this instruction given to you?

WITNESS: I recall it basically, but what I can remember is that the docket must go to the Director of Public Prosecutions, Your Worship.

DEFENCE LAWYER: I have shown this copy to my learned friend and he has not seen anything that directs you to take the docket to the DPP, and it is not there.

WITNESS: Your Worship, maybe if I can see that because I remember you said, yes, the docket must then go to the DPP, Your Worship.

DEFENCE LAWYER: Before I can give it to you, I put it to you that it is not there that…

COURT: Now you are being unfair to the witness. Really, if you want to make those allegations, then you have to show it to the witness and you haven't even showed it to the Court either.

DEFENCE LAWYER: As the Court pleases, Your Worship. Let me show it to the witness and then I will show the Court.

COURT: Yes.

WITNESS: Your Worship, I agree it is not written there. The docket was then sent to the Director of Public Prosecutions.

DEFENCE LAWYER: Can I show it to the Court, Your Worship?

COURT: Yes. Are you going to hand that in as an exhibit?

DEFENCE LAWYER: Yes, Your Worship, I intend doing so.

COURT: That will be Exhibit C.

DEFENCE LAWYER: Do you agree with me, Warrant Officer Lesley, that the instructions to investigating officers are written down by the Public Prosecutor.

WITNESS: That is correct, Your Worship.

DEFENCE LAWYER: But you still maintain that there was such an instruction for you to take the docket to the DPP?

WITNESS: Your Worship, it is possible that it could be after that instructions were completed. The norm is we give the docket to the Prosecutor here. The Prosecutor either makes a decision or not or instructs us that or requests us to send the docket to the DPP. Your Worship, I think that, because it is a senior officer in the Police that the Public Prosecutor didn't want to make a decision regarding it and then that the docket… I remember that I made a draft a memorandum that was signed by my commander and the docket was then sent to the DPP, Your Worship.

DEFENCE LAWYER: I put it to you, Mr Lesley, that you at all times had some scores to settle against the accused?

WITNESS: No, Your Worship. If you are an officer in the Police… I work closely with LCRC. I never had any hard feelings against the member or the office.

DEFENCE LAWYER: And that is why you even defied the instructions of the Public Prosecutor.

WITNESS: I did not defy, Your Worship. If you can see on that form there is indication that I made with my handwriting about what was done, Your Worship.

DEFENCE LAWYER: According the accused, the procedure is that, if the accident happened in a certain area or jurisdiction, photographers of that area must visit the scene. Bedford Area is serviced by photographers of Fort Beaufort police. Why did you prefer Warrant Officer de Klerk, who was on duty for Grahamstown cases only?

DEFENCE LAWYER: Okay. If you have no explanation, let us get back now to the procedures. I assume you were in the Police Services for some time. When a case is initiated, the accused is informed of such case and that you have got evidence against him.

WITNESS: Yes, Your Worship.

DEFENCE LAWYER: Also what rights he has regarding this case?

WITNESS: Yes. After the docket came back from the Director of Public Prosecutions, a J157 was issued with the charge sheet attached. That was then handed over to the accused in court, Your Worship, where the charge was then precisely explained to him, when it was drafted by the director of Public Prosecutions, Your Worship, to look at his interest. Your Worship, we did not take any statement from him.

COURT: Yes, but Mr Lesley, what I am trying to ascertain is on the day, you said you gave him a warning statement. When did you issue that warning statement? When was that issued?

WITNESS: Your Worship, if I can look I can give you the precise date that I took it.

COURT: Because, If I understand the question, you are saying that the warning statement was issued to him regarding the reckless and negligent driving, and that was after you found out about Bedford. Is that correct?

DEFENCE LAWYER: That is my question, Your Worship

COURT: So, why was the accused never informed of that, although you already had information and had visited the second scene?

WITNESS: Your Worship, at that stage I could not with certainty say that the evidence that I picked up there was of that motor vehicle, Your Worship. Before, I would have warned him to say, listen this is the case against you. I would rather want the evidence, Your Worship. If it came back negative, there was no need for me to warn him regarding that, Your Worship. So that is why I never warned him to say defeating the ends of justice or fraud, because I wasn't sure that there was evidence at that stage, Your Worship.

DEFENCE LAWYER: Mr Lesley, let us take it step by step. You have just told the Court that when there is a case against the accused it is very important that he must be informed and the importance about it is that he must be given and be informed of the rights that are involved. He was being warned of the reck and neck on the N2 road.

WITNESS: Your Worship, like I said, at that stage the only evidence I had against the accused was that of reck and neck. I did not have evidence to say that he was involved in fraud or any other cases, Your Worship. So, when I took the statement, the warning statement from him, he was warned regarding the evidence that I had against him.

DEFENCE LAWYER: Can I take that your answer, a very short one, is that you did it in respect of the N2 collision; that is in short? The warning statement that is in the docket was of the N2 collision?

WITNESS: Your Worship, yes.

DEFENCE LAWYER: And that warning statement procedurally is done before the docket is taken to the Public Prosecutor?

WITNESS: That is correct, Your Worship.

DEFENCE LAWYER: Yet the accused is today facing a charge of fraud. When was that being done?

WITNESS: Your Worship, he was only informed of the charge of fraud when a J175 summons was issued on him.

COURT: Mr Lesley, do you only issue a warning statement to a suspect when the Prosecutor instructs you to do that?

WITNESS: No, Your Worship. If there is evidence in a docket…

COURT: I was under the impression that when a person is arrested, then a warning statement is given to them.

WITNESS: That is correct, Your Worship.

COURT: Or rather, when the charge, sorry, when they are charged?

WITNESS: No, no, Your Worship. When there is a case against a person, there is evidence to say, say for example, Your Worship, let us take an assault case where Piet says Jan assaulted him. He will warn Jan that he has got a right to remain silent and everything, and then if he makes a statement regarding that, it can be used against him in a court of law.

COURT: So, do you only issue a warning statement once you get a decision from a prosecutor?

WITNESS: No, Your Worship. We do that before the time, Your Worship.

DEFENCE LAWYER: Yes, that is exactly my question. He is today facing a charge of fraud, but has a warning statement been taken from him in respect of that charge?

WITNESS: No statement has been taken from the person where he can answer or make a report regarding the charge of fraud, Your Worship.

DEFENCE LAWYER: Any reason why such an important step was not done?

WITNESS: Your Worship, we were looking after the interests of the accused, Your Worship. That is why we didn't take a statement from him, Your Worship.

DEFENCE LAWYER: In what sense?

WITNESS: Because, when you take a statement from a person and he makes any statement regarding that, it can and will be used against the person in a court of law. Seeing the seriousness of the charge of fraud or defeating the ends of justice I did not take the statement from the accused, so as to not let him incriminate himself if he was going to do that or (inaudible) himself.

COURT: So, if I understand your evidence, once the summons was issued for the fraud, you didn't take a warning statement from him?

WITNESS: No, Your Worship.

DEFENCE LAWYER: Because you were thinking of his best interests?

WITNESS: Your Worship, I was looking after his interests. Why would I make a statement if he is already going to be charged for that thing? Let him rather speak to his lawyer and we go to court and he can testify in court.

DEFENCE LAWYER: Okay. Do you now realise that his Constitutional rights have been severely prejudiced?

WITNESS: I don't think so, Your Worship

DEFENCE LAWYER: But he has not placed his version even before the DPP who made the decision.

WITNESS: Your Worship, he did apply for copies of the docket. No representation to my knowledge was made to the Public Prosecutor to change the decision, or the DPP to change his decision, Your Worship.

DEFENCE LAWYER: Mr Lesley, this is the point I am making. The accused has got a right to make a statement if he so wishes and to decline to do so, if he so wishes. But he must be given that right, do you agree with me?

WITNESS: That is correct, Your Worship.

DEFENCE LAWYER: And I am saying that in this instance he has not been given that right.

WITNESS: Your Worship, maybe if I can explain it like this. My feeling is what is worth against the accused if he is going to make a statement that he can incriminate himself than rather to remain silent and that why I thought it was the best decision for him not to make a statement, Your Worship.

DEFENCE LAWYER: Thank you for the explanation that I did not need. The point I am making is that he was not given the right to choose whether to make a statement or not before the charge of fraud was preferred against him.

WITNESS: Your Worship, if I didn't give him the right I made it in his best interests, Your Worship.

DEFENCE LAWYER: Now, lastly on this point, do you now realise that the Director of Public Prosecutions made a decision against the accused without having laid hands on the accused's version insofar as the fraud is concerned?

COURT: Just go back one line on that screen. It has gone blank there. The clerk must be a little bit more awake, please. Are you sleeping? That is a number of times it has gone off.

WITNESS: Yes, Your Worship. The decision and why the Director of Public Prosecutions made that decision...

WITNESS: I can't answer regarding that, Your Worship.

DEFENCE LAWYER: No, that is not what I am asking. Do you realise that a decision has been made against him without his version being heard, as it is supposed to be?

WITNESS: Your Worship, I can say the evidence in the docket is the decision made on. If he didn't make a statement regarding that, Your Worship, that is the evidence that was for the director...

DEFENCE LAWYER: Okay, I am going to leave this point. I will argue it at the end of the day. I will argue further that you are refusing to answer this question. But let us go on. Who is the complainant in this case of fraud?

WITNESS: Your Worship, the case before the Court is a simple one. There is a case of reck and neck that was opened and I was investigating it.

DEFENCE LAWYER: Mr Lesley I don't want to go around in circles. Just answer the question. Who is the complainant in this case of the fraud?

WITNESS: Your Worship, it was the State, Your Worship.

DEFENCE LAWYER: Okay. What is the CAS number of the case of fraud?

WITNESS: CAS Number of fraud is 648/2 and is the case here, Your Worship.

DEFENCE LAWYER: 648/2/10. Is it not the same as the one of the reck and neck in respect of the N2 collision?

WITNESS: That is correct, Your Worship.

DEFENCE LAWYER: Oh. It is the same?

WITNESS: That is correct, Your Worship.

DEFENCE LAWYER: Okay. Doesn't that mean, therefore, that there was no case specifically opened for fraud?

WITNESS: There was no docket opened, Your Worship.

DEFENCE LAWYER: For the fraud?

WITNESS: It is the same docket as the one for the reck and neck, Your Worship.

DEFENCE LAWYER: Okay, so instead of the reck and neck being further investigated, the whole thing was changed to fraud?

WITNESS: Your Worship, the reck and neck was investigated as well as the fraud charge, Your Worship, or my impression at that stage was defeating, Your Worship.

DEFENCE LAWYER: Now, when you got the information from the faceless individual that you do not want to disclose here, that the collision might have taken place on the Bedford road, you simply decided to go with Warrant Officer de Klerk?

WITNESS: Yes. I requested to go with him.

DEFENCE LAWYER: Okay, Warrant Officer Lesley. You did not know exactly where the collision took place on the Bedford road?

WITNESS: No, I was not sure and the informer didn't tell me the exact place.

DEFENCE LAWYER: And you also did not know where you were heading to with Warrant Officer de Klerk?

WITNESS: Only on the Bedford road. That was the information.

DEFENCE LAWYER: So, when you entered the Bedford road you started to look around throughout?

WITNESS: As we were driving, I was looking for any signs that there might have been an accident, Your Worship.

DEFENCE LAWYER: And when you were on the Bedford road, looking around, the faceless individual was not with you?

WITNESS: No, Your Worship.

DEFENCE LAWYER: You looked around until you got to a spot where you suspected this must be the spot?

WITNESS: That is correct, Your Worship.

DEFENCE LAWYER: Warrant Officer, this whole exercise was against the basic rights of the accused in that at the end he was going to be charged for fraud.

WITNESS: Your Worship, at that stage I was just following information. If it was not true, we wouldn't be here, Your Worship

DEFENCE LAWYER: Yes, exactly on that point, and the whole exercise was intended to go against the basic rights of the accused.

WITNESS: Your Worship, my understanding is it is information I have to follow up. I followed it up and I was done, Your Worship.

DEFENCE LAWYER: Even when you followed it up without his knowledge, when you got the information, again you did not inform the accused?

WITNESS: Your Worship, like I said, I would only confront the accused if I have got evidence against that accused, Your Worship.

DEFENCE LAWYER: So, you don't want to agree that you did not inform the accused.

WITNESS: I only informed the accused of the evidence that I had against him. I did not inform him of any speculation. That was because I don't think it was needed at that stage, Your Worship

DEFENCE LAWYER: Let us just follow it up... (interrupted)

COURT: I just want to follow your line of questioning again. Are you saying that the police are supposed to inform an accused person of what is going on in the investigation every step of the way?

DEFENCE LAWYER: That is not what I am saying.

COURT: Then what are you trying to say?

DEFENCE LAWYER: I am saying that when they get information about the accused, then they must inform the accused and give the accused the right to make a statement if he so wishes.

COURT: Yes, you have made your point regarding the fact that he was not warned on that statement with regards to the fraud, so can you move on?

DEFENCE LAWYER: As the Court pleases. Now, you called on the photographer on the day in question?

WITNESS: There are two that I requested to help me. One is Van Onselen and one is De Klerk, yes.

DEFENCE LAWYER: In respect of the Bedford road…

WITNESS: Yes, Warrant Officer de Klerk requested to go with me to take photographs if needed.

DEFENCE LAWYER: And some pointing out was made in the process of the photographer working?

WITNESS: Yes. Those are observations I made and he took photographs of that, Your Worship.

DEFENCE LAWYER: And you were pointing some issues out to the photographer?

WITNESS: I pointed to stuff there, Your Worship, yes.

DEFENCE LAWYER: It is not the person who knew where the collision took place who pointed out? It is you, having been told?

WITNESS: That is correct, Your Worship. It is me on the photos and I pointed out the stuff that I saw there, Your Worship.

DEFENCE LAWYER: Any reason why your faceless informer was not the one who was pointing out the spots on the scene?

WITNESS: He was not there, Your Worship.

DEFENCE LAWYER: Any reason why he was not called to make the pointing out?

WITNESS: Your Worship, If I have got to ask any person to give information and to be pointing on a photograph the people won't bring information to the police. That is why I didn't take him, Your Worship.

DEFENCE LAWYER: Remember, the accused was not there.

WITNESS: That is correct, Your Worship.

DEFENCE LAWYER: So, it would been yourself and the informer and Van Onselen, rather the photographer.

WITNESS: But it was just me and De Klerk who was there, Your Worship.

DEFENCE LAWYER: So, you were pointing out some spots that were told to you and not pointed to you by the informer?

WITNESS: No, Your Worship. The points that I pointed out there were what I had observed on the scene, Your Worship.

COURT: How did you come about that scene? Were you just driving along and came upon it, or did your informer tell you exactly where to go?

WITNESS: The informer didn't say. He said only on the Bedford road, Your Worship. He didn't say it was five kilometres or ten kilometres or fifty kilometres. We just drove. If I'd got to Bedford and I didn't see anything, I would have turned back and that would have been the end.

DEFENCE LAWYER: Now, you told the Court that you went back to the office and sealed the pieces of evidence that you obtained from the scene?

WITNESS: Your Worship, the property that I picked up on the Bedford road I sealed on the Bedford road, Your Worship.

DEFENCE LAWYER: Okay...

WITNESS: The property that was placed in exhibit bags that I found on the N2 was sealed on the N2, except if it was too big for the exhibit bag.

DEFENCE LAWYER: Let us concentrate on the Bedford road. Having sealed them on the Bedford road, you then took them back to the office?

WITNESS: That is correct, Your Worship.

DEFENCE LAWYER: Okay. What did you do with them when you got back to the office?

WITNESS: I then placed them in my steel cabinet and then the next morning I went and compared with the motor vehicle.

DEFENCE LAWYER: Okay. Having made some comparisons, you took some pieces from the motor vehicle?

WITNESS: Yes, I requested a mechanic to cut out a piece of the bumper, which I then sent down to the lab, Your Worship.

DEFENCE LAWYER: And that is exactly what you did?

WITNESS: Your Worship, also like I said, I observed the motor vehicle itself.

DEFENCE LAWYER: I am instructed by the accused that the procedure is that, when the exhibits are obtained from the scene, then they are recorded in a specific register at the police station.

WITNESS: That is correct, Your Worship. Later the exhibits... excuse me that I did not send away... were then booked into the SAPS13.

DEFENCE LAWYER: Okay. But you were telling the Court that those that you later sent to Port Elizabeth were not entered at all in the register?

WITNESS: That is correct, Your Worship. It was kept under my custody and it was locked up by me, Your Worship.

DEFENCE LAWYER: Why was it so?

WITNESS: Your Worship, it is practically... I know I am going to be the person who is going to pack it and have it sent away, then I have got to get a statement of the SAP13 clerk. I have to get a statement of the person who was working in the charge office. It is for the chain of evidence to be easier, so I kept it with me, Your Worship.

DEFENCE LAWYER: Your Worship, can I just take an instruction?

COURT: Yes.

DEFENCE LAWYER: I am instructed, Warrant Officer, that the truth is that the pieces of evidence that you are talking about from the Bedford road collision were in fact entered into an SAP13 register.

WITNESS: That is correct. That is what I said, Your Worship, except the part that I sent down the lab, Your Worship.

DEFENCE LAWYER: Okay. If I remember well, what you sent to the lab were the pieces from the motor vehicle?

WITNESS: That is correct, Your Worship, and if I can refer to the photograph to make it clear, Your Worship?

COURT: You sent some pieces of the motor vehicle that you found in Bedford, plus the one that you took from the motor vehicle?

WITNESS: That is correct, Your Worship. That is the piece I took that we cut out. It is what I point to at paragraph 44 of the album.

DEFENCE LAWYER: And everything else was then left in the police station?

WITNESS: The other exhibits that were picked up were then handed over in to SAP13 also, except the blood that was handed in later, Your Worship.

DEFENCE LAWYER: Okay. May the Court just bear with me, Your Worship.

COURT: So, if I understand your evidence, the parts that you kept in the safe, those were later handed to whom?

WITNESS: Also handed in to the SAP13, Your Worship.

COURT: The ones that were in the safe?

WITNESS: The ones that were in the safe.

COURT: You said you sent them to the lab?

WITNESS: No, no, Your Worship. The ones that were in the safe were the exhibits that I picked up on the N2. All those exhibits I booked into the SAP13, except the blood that I picked up there. That was sent to the lab, but it came back and was not analysed, Your Worship. The only exhibits that I kept with me that I didn't book into the SAP13, Your Worship, is the plastic piece that I pointed out in the photo 44, Your Worship, and then the one that I picked up on the Bedford road, Your Worship, is the plastic piece that I pointed out in the photo 44, Your Worship, and then the one that I picked up on the Bedford road, Your Worship.

COURT: What did you do with that?

WITNESS: I sealed it in another big security bag, Your Worship, and it was taken then down to the lab by Sergeant Oosthuizen.

COURT: Yes, that is what I am trying to figure out… So, apart from yourself, it was who else who had access to those exhibits apart from yourself?

WITNESS: Only myself, Your Worship.

COURT: And then you gave it to Mr Oosthuizen, who took it to the lab?

WITNESS: Sergeant Oosthuizen, yes, to take it after it was sealed in a bigger bag, Your Worship.

DEFENCE LAWYER: Your Worship, just before I go past this point, let me have a minute with the accused?

COURT: Yes.

DEFENCE LAWYER: Thank you, Your Worship. Now, you told the Court that you asked a mechanic to go and cut some pieces from the motor vehicle?

WITNESS: That is correct, Your Worship.

DEFENCE LAWYER: When did you do that?

WITNESS: If I remember correctly, it was round about a couple of days after I sent it down to the lab, so around about the 7th or 8th of March.

DEFENCE LAWYER: Are you sure?

WITNESS: That is correct, Your Worship, because I know the stuff was taken down to the lab on the 10th, Your Worship.

DEFENCE LAWYER: Just a minute, Your Worship. And when you were asking the mechanic to go and do that, again the accused was not aware…

WITNESS: Your Worship, I don't think it was necessary for me to inform the accused I was going to do that, Your Worship.

DEFENCE LAWYER: Now, having started the investigations, Warrant Officer, about the Bedford collision on the 1st of March, was the motor vehicle itself secured or guarded by anybody so that nobody interferes with it, as at the 10th?

WITNESS: Your Worship, that vehicle was parked at the VIS ground, the vehicle safeguarding unit, outside which has got guards.

DEFENCE LAWYER: Now, let us get back to the scene on the Bedford road. You say the only reason why you formed the opinion that the collision must have taken place at the Bedford road is that you saw a spot of blood; a big spot of blood?

WITNESS: Your worship, if I remember correctly, I said my opinion was that the collision with an animal took place there.

DEFENCE LAWYER: And it is your observations there…

WITNESS: …that there was an accident with an animal, Your Worship

DEFENCE LAWYER: And you happened to be so lucky as well to see the intestines of an animal on the spot?

WITNESS: Your Worship, I pointed it out in a photograph how far from the spot it was laying, Your Worship.

DEFENCE LAWYER: Okay. Did you perhaps, or is there any reason why you did not, find the carcass of the animal itself on the scene?

WITNESS: Your worship, I did go and do enquiries round in the area, Your Worship, and I was informed that late on the Friday night there were lights and everything. I presume some other people took the animal away, Your Worship. But I didn't see an animal on the scene when I arrived there, Your Worship.

DEFENCE LAWYER: Who gave you the information that on the night there were some lights there?

WITNESS: I did go and do an enquiry at the farm workers who can see the road, the farm workers there at Malanskraal, if they know anything, saw anything. The only thing they could say is that there were lights there, Your Worship.

DEFENCE LAWYER: Okay, and according to the information that you got, those lights were there on the night before you went there on the 1st?

WITNESS: I said the Friday night; they saw it the Friday night there. I went on Monday there, Your Worship.

DEFENCE LAWYER: So you then assumed that people must have taken away the carcass?

WITNESS: I don't know who took it, or what happened to the carcass, Your Worship, but I suspected that is what happened, Your Worship.

DEFENCE LAWYER: I take it that was during summer?

WITNESS: It was February, summer, Your Worship.

DEFENCE LAWYER: And if the intestines were there as from 6 o'clock on the 26th as they were on the 1st, they might have been damaged by then?

WITNESS: Your Worship, like I explained, it was dry intestines. It was not wet, new, bloody intestines, Your Worship. So they could have been lying there for a couple of days, Your Worship.

DEFENCE LAWYER: But they were fortunately not devoured by the cannibals?

WITNESS: The photographs I took is what I got there, so luckily it wasn't taken.

DEFENCE LAWYER: That was indeed fortunate. Warrant Officer, I put it to you that at all times you had an axe to grind against the accused.

WITNESS: No, Your Worship.

DEFENCE LAWYER: I put it to you further that, if there are any intestines that you found at the Bedford road, those were planted by you.

WITNESS: Your Worship, I do not have reason to do something like that, Your Worship.

DEFENCE LAWYER: But you had all the reasons to investigate behind the back of the accused to the extent of not even giving him the right to make a warning statement?

WITNESS: Your Worship, until a report came back I was not certain that this vehicle was hundred percent involved in that collision, so before that time I don't want to make any allegations, especially against a senior officer, of fraud or defeating.

DEFENCE LAWYER: But even until today, you did not give the accused that right...

WITNESS: Like I said, I was under the impression that by not letting him make a statement I was looking after his rights, Your Worship.

DEFENCE LAWYER: Okay. Is it not the duty of the investigators to investigate and follow up information they get?

WITNESS: That is correct, Your Worship.

DEFENCE LAWYER: Is that what you consider to be prejudice, if you do it?

WITNESS: Your Worship, I don't understand prejudice, but I was not in favour of any other person except that I was doing my investigation, Your Worship.

DEFENCE LAWYER: Okay, let me put it this way: in what manner did you the investigators suffer prejudice by following up the information that you had?

COURT: I don't understand your question. What was the question?

DEFENCE LAWYER: Let me repeat my question, Your Worship. In what manner did you as the investigator suffer any prejudice by following up the information that you received about the Bedford collision?

WITNESS: Your Worship, I was not prejudiced in any way. I was investigating a case. In fact, actually if I was prejudiced I gave my (inaudible) light, otherwise it is my work. I have to follow up information. It doesn't matter where it leads me. It is what I have to do, Your Worship.

DEFENCE LAWYER: And anybody was prejudiced in any event by just following up the information?

WITNESS: No, Your Worship.

DEFENCE LAWYER: As the Court pleases, Your Worship. If before I resume my questions I can just approach the accused?

COURT: Yes.

DEFENCE LAWYER: You also made a statement, Warrant Officer?

WITNESS: That is correct, Your Worship.

DEFENCE LAWYER: In relation to the Bedford collision thing?

WITNESS: Yes I made a statement regarding the investigation that took place, Your Worship.

DEFENCE LAWYER: I want to show you this document. Take a look at it, in particular at the end of it.

WITNESS: That is correct, Your Worship.

DEFENCE LAWYER: Is that your signature appearing at the end of it?

WITNESS: That is correct.

DEFENCE LAWYER: Take a look at it, in particular at the end of it. Is that your signature appearing at the end of it?

WITNESS: That is correct, Your Worship.

DEFENCE LAWYER: Okay. Having looked at it as a whole, is it a statement that you made?

WITNESS: That is correct, Your Worship. There is only one typing error that happened here...

DEFENCE LAWYER: ...Where it says "On the 8th of August we went with Mr Goliath from the local garage and he saw off (I assume that must have been cut off) a piece of the bumper I indicated, placed it in security bag with number FSC218155 and sealed it". This is what appears in the statement.

WITNESS: Your Worship, that is what appears there and that is what I said is a typing error. It is supposed to be March not August.

DEFENCE LAWYER: Oh, it is March?

WITNESS: It is supposed to be March, Your Worship, yes.

DEFENCE LAWYER: Okay. You made a mistake?

WITNESS: It is a typing error, yes, Your Worship.

DEFENCE LAWYER: And you overlooked it when you were signing your statement?

WITNESS: That is correct, Your Worship. I picked this up later when I was going through the statements, Your Worship.

DEFENCE LAWYER: Okay. Do you happen to know as to when Mr Oosthuizen took the exhibits to the lab in Port Elizabeth?

WITNESS: If I remember correctly, it was the 10th of March I handed it over to him. He then took it after, whether it was the same day or the next day I am not a hundred percent sure, Your Worship.

NO FURTHER QUESTIONS BY THE DEFENCE LAWYER

Evidence by Warrant Officer Van Onselen

COURT:We will take the tea adjournment now. Court adjourns

COURT ADJOURNS AT 12H03

EVIDENCE ON BEHALF OF THE STATE

JOHANNES VAN ONSELEN

EXAMINATION BY PROSECUTOR

PROSECUTOR: Sir, you are employed by the South African Police Services?

WITNESS: I am a warrant officer in the South African Police, stationed at the Local Criminal Record Centre, Grahamstown.

PROSECUTOR: For how long have you been working for the Police Service?

WITNESS: As I said, I am warrant officer in the South African Police stationed at Grahamstown.

PROSECUTOR: For how long have you been working as a police officer, sir?

WITNESS: I have been working in the SAPS for eighteen years, where I have been working at the LCRC for seventeen years.

PROSECUTOR: What are you doing at the LCRC?

WITNESS: I am a fingerprint expert, official photographer, draughtsman, videographer and forensic fieldworker.

PROSECUTOR: Let us talk specifically, sir, regarding the... your duties as a photographer. Have you received any training as a photographer?

WITNESS: I was trained at the Criminal Record Centre training centre in Port Elizabeth, as well as Pretoria, in theory as well as the practical, which I passed. I have been doing that now for seventeen years.

PROSECUTOR: So, you have been working as a photographer for seventeen years?

WITNESS: That is correct, Your Worship.

PROSECUTOR: What type of incidents have you covered as a photographer?

WITNESS: I have covered incidents from assaults through to murders, armed robberies, motor vehicle accidents, everything that should be photographed by the SAPS I have photographed.

PROSECUTOR: Now, Sir, did you attend any scene of accidents?

WITNESS: On the 27th of the 2nd 2010, at approximately 08h30, I was requested by Superintendent Maqebhula to attend to a reckless and negligent driving case on the N2 road between Grahamstown and Port Elizabeth, approximately eighteen kilometres from Grahamstown, near the Alicedale, turning off the N2. The vehicle that was involved in the accident was photographed at the VIS Unit in Grahamstown. Afterwards, we proceeded to the scene on the N2 and on arrival I was approached by Mr Maqebhula who told me to stop at a certain scene, which he pointed, subsequently pointed, out to me.

PROSECUTOR: And you then took photographs of the scene?

WITNESS: I then took photographs of the scene. After making my own observations, I took photographs of the scene, that is correct.

PROSECUTOR: Do you see those photographs, sir?

WITNESS: Correct. These are the photographs that I took on the 27th of the 2nd 2010.

PROSECUTOR: Now, what type of camera did you use to take the photographs?

WITNESS: At the moment, we are using the digital cameras.

PROSECUTOR: Now, did you take those photographs yourself?

WITNESS: Yes, I did indeed do so.

PROSECUTOR: Can you take the Court through the photographs from photo B1 up to the last photo?

WITNESS: Okay, key to photo on EXHIBIT B before the Court, the reckless and negligent driving scene on the N2, approximately eighteen kilometres from Grahamstown on the Grahamstown road. It was attended on the 27th of February 2010, at approximately five past nine. The vehicle and certain points at the scene were indicated to me by Superintended Maqebhula. Photo 1 and 2, taken in an easterly direction, indicates the scene that allegedly took place on the N2 near the Alicedale turn off, as well as points A, B, C, D and E taken as photo 3, taken as a close up photo of point B, parts of the vehicle that were found on the scene

PROSECUTOR: Proceed, Sir.

WITNESS: Photo 4, taken as a close up photo of the alleged kudu blood found on the scene. Photo 4 to 10 taken of the damage to the vehicle DCG144EC.

PROSECUTOR: Where was this car at this stage?

WITNESS: At the VIS Unit, as I said earlier in my testimony, Your Worship. Photo 11 is taken of alleged kudu hair on the right-hand side mirror mount of the vehicle. Photo 12 taken of the kilometres reading of the vehicle at the time, DCG144EC at the VIS office, Grahamstown. Point A on the photographs indicates the alleged direction that the vehicle DCG144EC was travelling in towards Grahamstown when the kudu was hit. Point B on the photographs indicates parts of the vehicle DCG144EC that was found on the scene. Point C on the photos indicates possible kudu blood found on the scene. Point D on the photographs indicates the fixed-point marker N2-32 East. Point E on the photographs indicates where the vehicle DVG144EC allegedly came to a standstill after the accident. Distances are as follows: B to D is plus/minus 8.5 metres, D to E approximately forty-three metres and the left lane northern side width is 5.7 metres.

PROSECUTOR: Is that all, sir?

WITNESS: That is correct, Your Worship. That is my testimony.

NO FURTHER QUESTIONS BY PROSECUTOR

COURT: Mr van Onselen, you said that you were trained in forensics as a forensic field officer?

WITNESS: That is correct, Your Worship.

COURT: Is it part of your expertise to make an expert opinion or to arrive at an expert opinion regarding accident scene?

WITNESS: Your Worship, with all the training we did regarding accident scenes and reconstruction of accident scenes, we try and reconstruct them as close as possible to what the scene originally looked like and yes, with the eighteen-year experience I would say I could give an opinion. I won't say it is my expert opinion, but through experience and in the regard of the reconstruction of a scene and then commenting regarding those scenes.

COURT: And from your observation of the scene in question, what conclusion did you draw?

WITNESS: Your Worship, the scene in question, according to my eighteen years of experience did not look to me as if any animal was struck at that scene or that any accident did actually occur on that scene, Your Worship.

COURT: Why do you say so?

WITNESS: The reason for that being, Your Worship, firstly I saw the vehicle before we went out to the scene. I photographed the vehicle at the VIS Unit looking at the damage to the vehicle and the amount of blood. That blood had to go somewhere and for us, pointed as point C, one speck of blood like that would not be consistent with such an accident.

Secondly, Your Worship, as marked out as point B, the right -hand side rear view mirror outside of the vehicle was broken off. That mirror was found on the left-hand side of the road, on the grass. Your Worship, further, the panel coming, also marked as point B on the photographs, of photo 3, the grey panel in sight there comes off the left inside door window frame panel and when looking at photo 7 both the passenger, looking from the front of the vehicle, the right-hand side, the passenger front and back window were still intact and according to me it is no possibility for that to fall onto the scene from that position, seeing that the back window of the vehicle was also intact.

COURT: I take it you did not observe the scene at Bedford?

WITNESS: Your Worship, no, I never saw the alleged scene that they are talking about at Bedford, no.

COURT: And can you give me your qualification again?

WITNESS: Your Worship, trained fieldworker, forensics, fingerprint expert, official draughtsman, official photographer and video operator.

COURT: And all these are qualifications received from the SAP?

WITNESS: From the SAPS CRC Training Centre, Your Worship, yes, which then would put me as a criminalistics expert through all the training

CROSS EXAMINATION BY DEFENCE LAWYER

DEFENCE LAWYER: Warrant Officer, you are not an expert?

WITNESS: That is correct. I am not an expert photographer. I am a fingerprint expert. I am not a forensic expert and I am not an expert photographer. I am an official photographer, official draughtsman, fingerprint expert, forensic fieldworker and video operator as I have said in my testimony.

DEFENCE LAWYER: And you are not an accident reconstruction expert either?

WITNESS: I am an official photographer, draughtsman. So, in other words, reconstruction of crime scene, accident scene, we do officially for the SAPS.

DEFENCE LAWYER: As much as you do such things, would you then describe yourself as being an expert?

WITNESS: With seventeen years' experience of taking photographs and reconstruction of crime scenes, I would do so, yes, Your Worship.

DEFENCE LAWYER: But in your evidence you have just told the Court that you did observe the hair allegedly from the kudu?

WITNESS: Yes, I did, Your Worship.

DEFENCE LAWYER: And you also observed what was referred to you as blood?

WITNESS: Yes, Your Worship, but I did note, I did mention as well, the speck of blood that was on the scene.

DEFENCE LAWYER: Where exactly was this blood?

WITNESS: If you look at photo B1 and B2, Your Worship, you can actually see on the points as they have been marked, and that would then be point C.

DEFENCE LAWYER: My instructions are that the collision with the kudu took place exactly on the spot that the accused pointed to you.

WITNESS: Your Worship, that to me is very inconsistent. Firstly, as I have said, the amount of blood and damage to the vehicle, the amount of glass, the amount of blood that was found on the scene that was pointed out to me is inconsistent with that. Secondly, for only the lights to all be broken in the front, it seems as if you can see on the photographs on the left-hand side of the vehicle, including the flicker and the mirror, glass, that whole scene was inconsistent, as I have said in my testimony, Your Worship, with all those things not being present on the scene.

DEFENCE LAWYER: Where do you think the glass on the surface of the road and the blood could have come from?

WITNESS: The glass, blood as pointed out on photo 4, the blood was definitely placed on the scene, Your Worship. That was definitely not made from impact with a vehicle at the time of the collision.

DEFENCE LAWYER: Are you saying that, according to your observation, the blood was placed on the spot?

WITNESS: That is correct, Your Worship.

DEFENCE LAWYER: That is very important, do you agree with me?

WITNESS: I totally agree that the blood was placed on the scene as marked out in exhibit B, photo no 4. I totally agree that blood was placed, as you have just said, has been placed on that scene. That is quite correct, yes.

DEFENCE LAWYER: Yes. The point I am making is that information so important should have been placed on your statement.

WITNESS: Your Worship, as I have said in my testimony and to our learned friend, the blood on point C was definitely placed on the scene on the N2, approximately eighteen kilometres from Grahamstown near the Alicedale turn in.

DEFENCE LAWYER: That is not the question, Warrant Officer. Should I repeat my question?

WITNESS: Please do so, Your Worship.

DEFENCE LAWYER: I am saying that, according to your observations, the fact that the blood was placed on the scene is a very important piece of evidence and I would have thought that one should have placed it on the statement.

WITNESS: Your Worship, that is true. The blood was definitely placed on the scene, by who I am not sure, but it was definitely not where the accident occurred. The amount of blood and the consistency to the damage of the vehicle does not agree to the amount of blood found on the scene near the N2. The blood on the N2 was definitely placed there by someone. In actual fact, that is the scene that was pointed out to me by Superintendent Maqebhula, so he was the only one knowing where the scene would have been. So that is the only one that I can mention that could have possibly put the blood on the scene. I had no knowledge of where the scene was.

DEFENCE LAWYER: Thank you very much, Warrant Officer, for all this explanation. Did you get my question?

WITNESS: Yes I did, and that is the way I answered it, Your Worship.

DEFENCE LAWYER: Then answer the question if you can.

WITNESS: I have just answered the question, Your Worship.

DEFENCE LAWYER: Let me repeat: do you agree that the information that, according to your observations, the blood was placed on the spot is so important that one should have included it in one's statement?

WITNESS: Your Worship, as I have said in my key to my photographs as well, that scene was pointed out to me by Mr Maqebhula. I had no knowledge of where the scene was prior to that, but the blood in question – point C on photograph 4 was definitely placed on the scene near the Alicedale turn in. The only person who could have shown that to me was Mr Maqebhula when he pointed the scene out to me and that is the only way the blood could have got to the scene.

COURT: Mr Van Onselen, maybe, I don't know if you understood the question. His question is that this bit of information is very important. Do you agree with that or not?

WITNESS: That blood was placed on the scene? On this scene on the Alicedale, nearby the Alicedale road?

COURT: Yes. Do you admit that the piece of evidence is very important?

WITNESS: Alicedale turn in. Yes, it was placed there.

COURT: I am not saying that the blood was placed. I am saying that your conclusion that the blood was placed there is important evidence. Do you agree with that or not?

WITNESS: Yes. That is, I agree with that.

COURT: That is the question that he is asking you.

WITNESS: Sorry. I am actually Afrikaans, Your Worship, sorry, yes.

COURT: That is the question that is being asked.

WITNESS: I am just trying to please the Court.

COURT: Well, it would be better, if you are more comfortable in Afrikaans, if we have an Afrikaans interpreter.

WITNESS: Okay. That would be better. Thank You, Your Worship.

COURT: Yes, it will just avoid misunderstanding confusion, okay.

WITNESS: No, it is perfect. Thank you, Your Worship.

DEFENCE LAWYER: What is your answer? Is it that you agree that the information is very important?

WITNESS: I don't agree with what you are saying. I agree that this blood was placed on the scene. And there was blood on the scene.

COURT: Can you just ask the witness, does he agree that it is important evidence?

WITNESS: It could be important evidence, Your Worship.

DEFENCE LAWYER: You are on the fence now; please come up clean. What do you mean when you say it could be?

WITNESS: Your Worship, seeing that the blood is becoming such an issue, I mean it could be important evidence. Firstly, if you look at the damage to the vehicle, the amount of blood as I have said in my testimony, at point C on photo 4, is not consistent with any motor vehicle accident where an animal is involved and the amount of blood that was found on the scene on the N2 is not consistent, so yes, it could be important evidence, Your Worship.

DEFENCE LAWYER: Let me put it this way: you made a statement immediately after you attended the scene of the accident?

WITNESS: I did not make the statement immediately. I made the statement, if you can actually check on the dates when the album was compiled, the statement was made on the 24th of the 3rd 2010.

DEFENCE LAWYER: Yes, and that was less than a month after you attended the scene of the accident?

WITNESS: That is correct, Your Worship.

DEFENCE LAWYER: And at the time you made the statement, everything was still fresh in your mind?

WITNESS: That is correct, Your Worship, because we have got scene reports that we keep with our crime scene to have all your evidence and all your different markings of your scene intact so that you are able to make a statement of your scene that you visited on any specific date or time.

DEFENCE LAWYER: As an expert, according to you, there is nothing that prevents you from placing your opinion and observation on the statement when you do it?

WITNESS: Your Worship, my observation as I have said any scene gets observed by me before it is photographed and any observation I make will also be noted and or photographed.

DEFENCE LAWYER: So, am I correct or do I get you clearly to say there was nothing that was preventing you from clearly placing on your statement your observations?

WITNESS: No. The only thing I could do from my scene report I could only put on my statement what I found on my observations at the scene and any of those observations I would then put in my statement, Your Worship.

DEFENCE LAWYER: Yes, but did you place those observations in your statement?

WITNESS: Your Worship, as I have indicated on Exhibit B, that has been handed...

DEFENCE LAWYER: Take a look at this document and confirm if this is your statement?

WITNESS: That is correct, Your Worship.

DEFENCE LAWYER: And it is exactly the statement that you made less than a month from the day of the collision?

WITNESS: That is the statement that I made on the 24th of the 3rd 2010, Your Worship.

DEFENCE LAWYER: Now, on this statement, on this statement you did not mention your observation as you are doing in court now...

WITNESS: On the key to the photographs explaining the scene, Your Worship, it was mentioned.

DEFENCE LAWYER: Yes, but what is your answer to my question?

WITNESS: What are you asking?

DEFENCE LAWYER: I am saying that on the statement you did not mention your observation as you are doing it in court now.

WITNESS: Your Worship, as it says in the statement, if I may read it again, as well as the key to the photographs clearly states everything that I mentioned in my testimony now.

COURT: Since I haven't seen the statement, maybe you want to put to him what he hasn't mentioned.

DEFENCE LAWYER: As the Court pleases. In your statement, you have not mentioned specifically that according to your observations the blood that was on the surface of the road was placed on the scene...

WITNESS: The photographs, the key to the photographs, shows, indicates to me as well as my own observations as well in my statement after the indication and after I had made my own observations.

DEFENCE LAWYER: Do you want me to read the statement to you?

WITNESS: You may do that

DEFENCE LAWYER: Okay, I am going to read from paragraph 2, or rather let me start from 1:

"Johannes van Onselen states under Oath in English I am an inspector in the SA Police Service stationed at the Local Criminal Record Centre, Grahamstown, as a fingerprint expert and official draughtsman and photographer, a video operator as well as a forensic fieldworker. On the 27th of February 2010, at approximately 8h30, I was requested by Superintendent Maqebhula to attend to a reckless and negligent driving scene on the N2 about eighteen kilometres from Grahamstown on the Port Elizabeth road near Alicedale turn in to Grahamstown. The vehicle scene and certain points at the scene were pointed out to me by Superintendent Maqebhula at approximately five minutes past nine. According to these indications, and after I have made my own observations, I photographed the scene as well as the vehicle.

Paragraph 4. A key to the photos was compiled.

Paragraph 5. I confirm the key to the photos to be correct and that it forms part of this statement. I know and understand the contents of this declaration. I have no objection to taking the prescribed oath. I consider the prescribed oath to be binding on my conscience.

And the statement is then signed by you at the bottom.

Now, this is my question. Please, I beg you try to answer it this time. Why did you not place your observations, as you are doing in court today, in the statement?

WITNESS: Your Worship, as you see on point C on Exhibit D handed in before the Court, possible kudu blood found on the scene.

DEFENCE LAWYER: Sorry for that, Your Worship. Let me repeat: Why did you not place the information that you are now telling me and the Court on this statement?

WITNESS: Your Worship, point C, Exhibit B on the photographs indicates possible kudu blood found on the scene

DEFENCE LAWYER: Warrant Officer, you really don't want to answer my question...

WITNESS: I am answering your question, Your Worship.

DEFENCE LAWYER: I am asking you about the statement, please...

WITNESS: As you have just read, Your Worship, in the statement that our learned friend read so nicely to us, plus my own observations, everything was there said, I confirm the key in the photographs to be correct and to form part of the statement point.

DEFENCE LAWYER: So, although you have not placed it on the statement, we can find it on the key to the photographs? Is that what you are saying?

WITNESS: Your Worship, point 5 of the affidavit that our learned friend has just read. I confirm the key and photos to be correct and this forms part of the statement, so yes, it does form part of the statement.

DEFENCE LAWYER: Okay. Both in the statement and the key to the photo plan, where exactly does it appear that you have placed clearly your observations and opinion, in particular that the blood was placed on the scene?

WITNESS: Your Worship, as I said in my testimony, if you look at the damage to the vehicle from photographs 5 to photograph 10, the blood on the scene, indicated as point C on photo 4, is not consistent. The blood had to go anywhere, if an animal was struck so severely to cause the amount of damage on the vehicle, there is definitely going to be more blood on the scene. That had to be, or there would be more blood that had to go anywhere and the blood as marked out as a point C is not enough blood to coincide with the amount of damage on the vehicle and the amount of blood and in the vehicle.

DEFENCE LAWYER: Okay. So, in short, you agree that you never placed that information both on the statement and key to photo plan? One has to assume from the amount of blood? As it reads, point C photos indicate kudu blood found on the scene. I am going to leave this point and argue that you are refusing to answer my question. I put it to you, Warrant Officer, that what you are telling the Court today about the observations on the scene not being consistent with the collision with a kudu is nothing but an afterthought.

WITNESS: Your Worship, I tried to explain to our learned friend as clearly as possible, and also with the seventeen years of attending to accident scenes, where animals have been hit, this scene was not consistent with any kudu being hit on the scene. That is my opinion concerning the scene that was pointed out to me on the 27th of the 2nd 2010.

DEFENCE LAWYER: Yes, I hear that Warrant Officer, but I am putting it to you that you are coming with this as an afterthought. Can you comment on that?

WITNESS: Your Worship, I don't know how this could be an afterthought. I mean, the scene was pointed out by Mr Maqebhula to me, photographs taken and noted. How could it be now an afterthought? When he pointed the scene out to me, this is what I found at the scene, so I don't know what could just indicate slightly more but I don't see any afterthought involved in this at all. This was as was pointed out by the client.

DEFENCE LAWYER: Let me put it this way: did you raise this with the accused on the day in question?

WITNESS: After the accused was warned according to Judges Rules, everything was pointed out to me by him and according to those I took photographs and also made my own observations.

DEFENCE LAWYER: Warrant Officer, do you understand the English language perfectly...

WITNESS: This scene was photographed after being pointed out by the accused.

DEFENCE LAWYER: Warrant Officer, that is not my question. Did you get my question?

WITNESS: This is the question that was put to me and I did answer, yes.

DEFENCE LAWYER: Let me repeat the question, please, to save time of this court. You had your own observations on the scene. Did you raise these observations to Colonel Maqebhula at the time?

WITNESS: I couldn't because as he pointed the scene out, you actually see on photo 1 there is a man disappearing to the right of point C behind the bushes as he ran off the scene to talk on the cell phone, Your Worship, indicated on photo 1, so there was no chance. I mean to try and do anything like that. There, you can actually see the man walking off the scene behind the bushes to the right of point C.

COURT: Sorry, who is this person now that was walking?

WITNESS: The accused before the Court, Your Worship.

COURT: So you say.

WITNESS: After he pointed the scene out to me and I started putting out the cones to photograph the scene, he walked off the scene to the right there and as you can see just slightly appearing behind the bush there was a photograph taken with him disappearing behind the bush talking on the cell phone.

DEFENCE LAWYER: Do you then want the Court to accept that the only reason why you could not raise these things with him is because he was attending to the cell phone?

WITNESS: No, because that is what he pointed out to me, Your Worship. That is the scene as he pointed it out to me. I do not have to ask him to query about anything. That is what he wished to point out to me and that is what I photographed. This is his choice to say or do, point out anything on the scene, I mean, this is what he pointed out to me and this what I photographed.

DEFENCE LAWYER: So, in other words now, even if he had not attended to the cell phone, you would not have raised these things with him?

WITNESS: As I said, Your Worship, he indicated the scene to me and that was what was photographed.

DEFENCE LAWYER: That I understand…

WITNESS: And after, and even after it was photographed, what else must I find out about the scene? He gave me a clear indication of where he was allegedly coming from, where the kudu, alleged kudu, was allegedly struck, with the possible parts of the vehicle lying next to the road where he allegedly stopped after the incident, as well as then the fixed point that was marked out with a plastic bag. I don't have to ask him anything else. There, to me, that is more than enough evidence to take the photographs

COURT: Mr Van Onselen, when you observed the scene and you made your conclusion, did you arrive at the conclusion at the scene that the scene is not consistent with what Mr Maqebhula is saying?

WITNESS: That is correct, Your Worship.

COURT: Why did you not raise that issue with him at the scene?

WITNESS: Because, Your Worship, he obviously wanted me to believe that it happened at that certain scene and that is why I didn't raise anything further about that, concerning that scene. And seeing that he was my commander at this stage, one doesn't to get too involved in any argument further

DEFENCE LAWYER: So it was the both of you on the scene?

WITNESS: That is correct, Your Worship.

DEFENCE LAWYER: Now, you came back to the office?

WITNESS: On the Monday, Your Worship.

DEFENCE LAWYER: Yes, on Monday you came back to the office.

WITNESS: That is correct.

DEFENCE LAWYER: And when you made the statement, he was not next to you?

WITNESS: No, he wasn't next to me, Your Worship.

DEFENCE LAWYER: Now, if for the reason that he was your commander, that you did not want to have a conflict with him, why did you not then have it appearing on the statement, now that you are alone?

WITNESS: Excuse me, can you just, can you just repeat the question? I do not really understand now.

COURT: The question that he is trying to get is why did you not raise this issue before you came to court today. Why was it not put in any of your statements?

WITNESS: Because, Your Worship, it was put into my album as indicated on point C marked out in my key to the photos.

COURT: I think we have been through this, Mr Msindo. You are going around in circles now.

DEFENCE LAWYER: Yes, Your Worship, I understand that. Now, did you at any stage convey this information, perhaps to the Public Prosecutor?

WITNESS: I saw the Public Prosecutor this morning, before the Court.

DEFENCE LAWYER: Yes. The question is, did you convey this important information to him?

WITNESS: No reason for me to convey.

DEFENCE LAWYER: So, you did not even tell the Public Prosecutor during consultation about this?

WITNESS: Your Worship, I think our learned friend understands me incorrectly. I never said I consulted him.

DEFENCE LAWYER: Okay. You are telling the Court that before you stood here you did not even have a word with the Public Prosecutor?

WITNESS: We did not go through the content of the album, not at all. We did not go through the whole key to photographs as I read it out in court or the statement as I read it out in court. I did not go through that as I read it out. We did not go through. I barely mentioned that these are the photographs that I had taken.

DEFENCE LAWYER: Warrant Officer, who has asked you about going through the statement now?

WITNESS: It seems you did ask me now, did I consult him? I said no, well I didn't consult, seeing that I didn't go through the whole key to photograph as well as the statement, which I would see as consultation, which I didn't do. So no, I did not. I am mentioning the statement again and the key to the photographs again in my testimony on the question.

DEFENCE LAWYER: Okay. I am going to leave that one unanswered as well.

COURT: What is your question?

DEFENCE LAWYER: The question is whether he conveyed this information to my learned friend before getting to the witness box. That is my question.

COURT: Alright.

WITNESS: No, I did not convey anything because your learned friend had the album with him, so I did not convey any of the information to him.

DEFENCE LAWYER: Now, when you are there on the witness box being led by my learned friend, narrating the events, you did not mention that until you were asked by the Court.

WITNESS: Yes, as I went through the statement

NO FURTHER QUESTION BY DEFENCE LAWYER

CHAPTER ELEVEN

Evidence of Warrant Officer F de Klerk

EXAMINATION BY PROSECUTOR

PROSECUTOR: Sir, you are employed by the South African Police Services and stationed at Grahamstown Police Station, is that correct?

WITNESS: Dit is korrek

PROSECUTOR: For which unit are you working?

WITNESS: Ek werk by die Plaaslike Krieminele Rekord Sentrum.

PROSECUTOR: What exactly are you doing at the Criminal Record Centre?

WITNESS: Ek is 'n kriminalistieke deskundige, ek bedrywig met foto's, vingerafdrukke, plantekening, forensies.

PROSECUTOR: For how long have you been working for SAPS, especially under the unit that you are working in?

WITNESS: Nineteen years' service in the police and eighteen years in this one.

PROSECUTOR: You mentioned that you are also a photographer. Is that correct?

PROSECUTOR: Yes, I am also a photographer.

WITNESS: Do you have any qualification for being a photographer?

WITNESS: I was also trained by the Criminal Record Centre in Grahamstown and also the Criminal Record Centre in Pretoria.

PROSECUTOR: What qualification did you obtain?

WITNESS: Criminalistic expert certificate. I also obtain a certificate in that.

PROSECUTOR: Did you also do any practical training in order to get this certificate?

WITNESS: That is correct.

PROSECUTOR: For how long did you do practical training?

WITNESS: A portion of the training in Pretoria was also practical and then when you come back you are also spend some time doing some practical in Grahamstown.

PROSECUTOR: How many cases, if you can recall, have you attended as a photographer in which you had to take photographs, if you can recall?

WITNESS: Between five to fifteen per month in the last eighteen years.

PROSECUTOR: How many cases of reckless or negligent driving have you attended as a photographer?

WITNESS: It is very difficult because even this morning I attended three; no in the last week I did three.

PROSECUTOR: Now, Sir, did you on the 1st of March 2010 attended a scene where you had to take some photographs?

WITNESS: That is correct.

PROSECUTOR: Where was that?

WITNESS: On the national road between Grahamstown and Bedford.

PROSECUTOR: Okay. Who was with you?

WITNESS: I was with Inspector Lesley.

PROSECUTOR: Why did you have to go there to take photographs?

WITNESS: Because I was requested to go there with Inspector Lesley.

PROSECUTOR: Did you take photographs on that day?

WITNESS: I did take photographs on that day

PROSECUTOR: Where exactly?

WITNESS: Near the Malanskraal turn off on the Bedford Road.

PROSECUTOR: Your Worship, can I give him a copy?

COURT: Yes. That is Exhibit A before the Court. I do have a copy.

WITNESS: I do have a copy, Your Worship, if that is alright?

PROSECUTOR: Do you have a copy?

WITNESS: I do have a copy

PROSECUTOR: Can you look at the photographs that are in front of you and confirm if you were the person who took the photographs or not?

WITNESS: That is correct. I took these photographs.

PROSECUTOR: And when did you take those photographs?

WITNESS: On the 1st of March 2010.

PROSECUTOR: Was it on the day when you were asked by Inspector Lesley?

WITNESS: Yes, that is correct, except photo 44, 45 and 46 were done the following day at the VIS Unit

COURT: Well, then I don't believe it is necessary. You are just going to rehash all the evidence that Mr Lesley has already given us. Photo album is here, everything has been pointed out to us.

PROSECUTOR: Yes.

COURT: Then it will be Exhibit A that is in the admitted evidence.

NO FURTHER QUESTIONS BY PROSECUTOR

CROSS-EXAMINATION BY DEFENCE LAWYER

DEFENCE LAWYER: Thank you, Your Worship. Mr de Klerk, you said you are stationed at Grahamstown?

WITNESS: That is correct.

DEFENCE LAWYER: On this day in question, that being the 1st of March 2010, you were requested to attend the scene at Bedford...

WITNESS: As we left here we were not sure where exactly where the place is as we were leaving Grahamstown.

DEFENCE LAWYER: Yes, but that is an explanation. I am just asking...

COURT: Just translate his question, please.

DEFENCE LAWYER: You have already given an explanation; I have not asked that. On this day you were requested to attend a scene at Bedford?

WITNESS: That is incorrect. No, sir, I was requested to attend on the Bedford road not in Bedford.

DEFENCE LAWYER: Is there a part of the Bedford road that falls within the jurisdiction of Grahamstown?

WITNESS: That is correct.

DEFENCE LAWYER: And when you were requested, Warrant Officer Lesley did not tell where exactly on the Bedford road?

WITNESS: No.

DEFENCE LAWYER: Let me leave that. I will come back to it later. You were going there to take photographs?

WITNESS: That is correct.

DEFENCE LAWYER: We have evidence on record to say on the very same day Warrant Officer Lesley was together with another photographer by name of Van Onselen.

COURT: No, that is not the evidence on record. He said that Van Onselen took the photos on the N2 and he took Mr de Klerk with him to Bedford.

DEFENCE LAWYER: Okay, I am sorry for that. Thank you for that, Your Worship. Do you perhaps know if Van Onselen attended the scene on the N2 road together with Lesley on that day? Let me repeat, I am sorry about, that Your Worship. Do you perhaps know if Warrant Officer van Onselen, on the 1st of March 2010 did attend a scene on the N2 road together with Lesley?

WITNESS: I have no knowledge of that.

DEFENCE LAWYER: Okay, now let us move on. You then happened to know where exactly the scene was when you were together with Lesley?

WITNESS: I didn't know where the scene was until I was shown it.

DEFENCE LAWYER: Okay, having been shown where the spot was, can you tell the Court if that spot was within the jurisdiction of Grahamstown or Bedford Police?

WITNESS: It was in the jurisdiction of Bedford Police.

DEFENCE LAWYER: Okay, and you came to know that before you could take the photos at the scene?

WITNESS: Yes, that is correct.

DEFENCE LAWYER: Okay, what is the procedure with the police? Is it normal that another police officer can go and do some duties in another jurisdiction?

WITNESS: If the investigation begins in your area, you must do it. Say it is from here to Bloemfontein, you have to go up there.

DEFENCE LAWYER: So, your short answer is that police officers do jobs in a different jurisdiction?

WITNESS: My answer is that, if your investigation begins or starts in Grahamstown, you start in Grahamstown up to the end.

DEFENCE LAWYER: Where did the investigation start?

WITNESS: It started in Grahamstown.

DEFENCE LAWYER: Okay, and when such investigations were started, Van Onslen was the photographer who attended the scene?

COURT: I don't think he knows anything about Mr Van Onselen.

DEFENCE LAWYER: Is it correct... I am instructed, I am instructed that when a police officer leaves the office to attend a particular complaint an entry in the pocketbook is made.

WITNESS: That is correct.

DEFENCE LAWYER: Warrant Officer de Klerk, yesterday when we adjourned, you had just told the Court that you did not record in your pocketbook the place you were departing for and the case number for the reason that Warrant Officer Lesley advised you not to bring the issue to the public knowledge until the whole information was obtained? But you did allude to the fact that Warrant Officer Lesley advised you not to bring the issue about the case to the public knowledge until the whole information is obtained.

WITNESS: I am sorry, Warrant Officer Lesley, I am sorry for that. He said that because he was afraid of the tampering with the evidence.

DEFENCE LAWYER: The point I am interested in is you were advised not to bring it to the public knowledge?

WITNESS: That is correct.

DEFENCE LAWYER: Now tell the Court, at what time did you receive the request to assist Warrant Officer Lesley?

WITNESS: It was after 14h00 when we left, just after 14h00, so I received it probably about half an hour before.

DEFENCE LAWYER: How was the request made to you by Warrant Officer Lesley?

WITNESS: I cannot remember if it was telephonically or in person. It would have been verbally.

COURT: Sir, can you just stick to one language?

DEFENCE LAWYER: Procedurally, at what stage does one make an entry into the pocketbook?

WITNESS: Is it a stage just before departure or when one comes back?

DEFENCE LAWYER: When you are leaving? Just before you depart?

WITNESS: When you are leaving.

DEFENCE LAWYER: In other words, before you left your station you had already spoken to Warrant Officer Lesley about this?

WITNESS: That is correct.

DEFENCE LAWYER: And that is when he told you that, look, please keep it a secret until you get the whole information about this?

WITNESS: No.

DEFENCE LAWYER: When did he tell about that?

WITNESS: On the stage where on the scene we picked up some parts. Then we found that those parts can possibly come from that vehicle, from that car. That is when he told me that it must not be public knowledge until he knows everything about those parts that we picked up there.

DEFENCE LAWYER: If I get you correctly, you were told to keep it a secret at the scene?

WITNESS: That is correct.

DEFENCE LAWYER: Now, if you were told at the scene, any reason why you did not enter it in your pocketbook? The case number, the name of the complainant, the place you were proceeding to? Let me repeat it: As you were leaving the office, just before you were told to keep it a secret, any reason why you did not place the CAS Number in pocketbook, the name of the complainant?

WITNESS: Not at departure, but he told me at the place of the scene.

DEFENCE LAWYER: Exactly. I understand you.

WITNESS: I did say that I took my pocketbook to that Bedford road.

COURT: Sorry, what is your question again?

DEFENCE LAWYER: The question is, he was told by Warrant Officer Lesley at the scene to keep everything secret about this matter until the whole information is obtained. Why did he not, when he left the office before he was told, make the correct entries in the pocketbook, to say I am leaving for this particular place. This is the CAS number and this is the complainant.

COURT: Okay, I think that I understand your question. Your question is why did he not make an entry with the CAS number in the pocketbook before he left to the scene? The answer to that was that he was told by Mr Lesley to keep it secret.

DEFENCE LAWYER: Exactly, that is my point Your Worship. Let me explain this. The answer that we got from the witness is that he was told by Warrant Officer Lesley to keep it a secret and he was told nowhere else, but at the scene that is on the Bedford road.

COURT: Oh, so you are saying, why did he not say that in the beginning?

DEFENCE LAWYER: The question is, when he left, before he could reach the scene...

COURT: I now understand your question

DEFENCE LAWYER: Thank you, Worship. The procedure is that you take the pocketbook and you write everything in the scene. Arrived at the scene at such time.

WITNESS: During the procedure there is no stage when you say that, can write that, I am leaving to such scene and such CAS number. Your write everything on the scene.

DEFENCE LAWYER: Do I get you correctly that it is only when you are on the scene that you enter the pocketbook that you are leaving for the scene that you are already in? Is that what you are saying?

WITNESS: Can you repeat the question?

DEFENCE LAWYER: Do I get correctly to say it is only when you are at the scene that you make an entry into the pocketbook that you are leaving for the scene that you are already in...?

WITNESS: No, that is incorrect.

DEFENCE LAWYER: What are you saying?

WITNESS: When I am leaving, I am writing in my pocket that I am leaving for such and such a place.

DEFENCE LAWYER: Yes.

WITNESS: Then I arrive on the scene, then I make a time of arrival. I do my investigation and finish. Before I leave there, then I write in my pocketbook what happened there and the CAS number.

DEFENCE LAWYER: Before you leave the office?

WITNESS: The scene.

DEFENCE LAWYER: Let us get back to the stage when you leave the office. Is it your evidence that when you leave the office you make an entry into your pocketbook that I am now leaving the office for a particular stage.

WITNESS: Yes, with the address.

DEFENCE LAWYER: And also you make an entry that I am leaving the office for a particular CAS number and that is when you are leaving the office?

WITNESS: No, there is no stage in my pocket I write that I am leaving for CAS number. I am just writing when I make an entry that I am leaving to such and such a place, but not a CAS number.

DEFENCE LAWYER: Let us follow that as well. Did you in your entry in your pocketbook make an entry that you are now leaving for Bedford road?

WITNESS: If I can look at that because I have already mentioned yesterday that my pocketbook is not available. As you can look further that in other cases that I attended I wrote where I went to. If you can look further down there…

DEFENCE LAWYER: You wrote where?

WITNESS: The other cases which I did earlier on that day I did write.

DEFENCE LAWYER: I am sorry, Warrant Officer. I am not interested at all about other cases.

WITNESS: I am trying to answer your question…

DEFENCE LAWYER: Not in relation to other cases. Answer my question in relation to what I am asking in this particular case.

WITNESS: I am saying to you that the reason that I did not do it is because I did not do it in other cases for the rest of the day.

DEFENCE LAWYER: Okay. So it means on that day you were breaking the procedures from the start of the day to the end?

WITNESS: I do not think that I even write it on my pocketbook that where I depart to or where I am going to.

DEFENCE LAWYER: Okay. I put it to you that, even before you could depart for Bedford, you had discussed this issue with Warrant Officer Lesley and you were advised before leaving the police station to keep it secret. Even if you enter your entry in the pocketbook, do not say it to anybody?

WITNESS: That is not true because I am only testifying that at what time that he asked me that.

DEFENCE LAWYER: Okay. Now I am told by the accused that at some stages you were acting as the commander at the police station?

WITNESS: The police station? That is incorrect.

DEFENCE LAWYER: At the station where you are ...

WITNESS: Yes, at my branch. That is correct.

DEFENCE LAWYER: And from that I take it that you know the procedures very well.

WITNESS: That is correct

DEFENCE LAWYER: Now, in every case – and this must be within your knowledge as the acting commander at some stages – in every case that you are attending from your branch, the name of the complainant must appear before you can leave and it must appear in your pocketbook first. You must know who the complainant is before you can leave the office.

WITNESS: No, that is not true. We go several times to other cases without the CAS numbers.

DEFENCE LAWYER: Okay. As an experienced investigator in instances where the State is involved, somebody must act on behalf of the State and make a statement and say State as per so and so. Is that not a procedure?

WITNESS: Repeat your question.

DEFENCE LAWYER: In every case where the State is involved, somebody acts on behalf of the State and when a statement is made, the first statement it reads Warrant Officer so and so, or rather State as per Warrant Officer so and so?

WITNESS: My investigation is different from this one because I do not know what other investigators are doing in their dockets. Different branches.

DEFENCE LAWYER: And in your case you do not need the name of the complainant before you can proceed?

WITNESS: We can go without a name or a CAS number to the scene.

DEFENCE LAWYER: And when you are coming back from the scene, you need to know the name of the complainant then?

WITNESS: That is correct

DEFENCE LAWYER: Now, you are standing before Court today and this is a fraud case. Tell us who is the complainant in this fraud case?

WITNESS: My answer to that question might incriminate the accused before Court.

DEFENCE LAWYER: No, I do not think you get my question....

WITNESS: I get your question perfectly well. That is why I give that answer. I get it perfectly well.

DEFENCE LAWYER: Oh, you do not want to incriminate the accused?

WITNESS: That is correct.

DEFENCE LAWYER: You have done so already. He is Court because of you.

WITNESS: I do not further want to incriminate him.

DEFENCE LAWYER: I am asking you, my brother. You are before Court on a fraud case. You have gone to the scene, made photos and everything. Who is the complainant in this case?

WITNESS: I understand your question I do not want to incriminate...

COURT: He does not want to answer that question. He says it is going to incriminate the accused further.

DEFENCE LAWYER: Your Worship, he can give me permission to answer that and say that because it will further incriminate the accused...

COURT: Do you want him to answer the question?

DEFENCE LAWYER: Yes. I am asking the question on instruction of the very accused. Please disclose, who is the complainant in the fraud case? As an experienced policeman, when a subpoena to attend any court case is issued, the accused is written there, so what was written in the place of accused?

WITNESS: At this stage, I do not know who the complainant is. It is in the docket and I cannot recall. I cannot recall it because my docket has been stolen or is missing because it was in the safe with the key and the accused knows about the key. The 14th March, and I also informed him that the docket has disappeared. I found out the docket was not there when I was looking for the album. Then after that I made further enquiries about the docket.

DEFENCE LAWYER: Next time when I ask you a question, just respond to the question without giving a lengthy explanation; just to save the Court's time. You understand me?

WITNESS: My opinion was that the answer is very important and it is my right to explain why I have to give that answer.

DEFENCE LAWYER: Now your answer is you do not know the complainant because the docket went missing. Is that what you are saying?

WITNESS: That is correct.

DEFENCE LAWYER: Otherwise, if the docket was in front of you, you would be able to know who the complainant is?

WITNESS: That is correct.

DEFENCE LAWYER: Okay. Before Court and on the basis on which this matter is proceeding, is a copy of the docket. Can I give it to you and you can point to us who the complainant is?

WITNESS: Is that docket mine? I have my own docket and the others have their dockets.

COURT: Of the same case?

WITNESS: That is correct.

DEFENCE LAWYER: Are you saying there are two dockets in the same case?

WITNESS: Correct. At the Criminal Record Centre, I make my own docket.

DEFENCE LAWYER: Okay.

WITNESS: The other branches make their own docket, so that is why I am asking whether the docket you are talking about is mine or the other branch docket?

DEFENCE LAWYER: Are you then telling the Court that the information that was in your own docket at the branch was never brought to the attention of the investigating officer for it to be part of the docket here?

COURT: Do you get the question, Warrant Officer?

DEFENCE LAWYER: Your Worship, with the greatest of respect, I am cross-examining the witness

COURT: Yes, sir, but you are putting something to the witness that he has not said you can argue.

DEFENCE LAWYER: Okay, now I understand you. Now, in your experience, you can answer that if you can, is it not procedural that in the docket before Court there must be a founding statement wherein the name of the complainant appears?

WITNESS: I have just testified that I never worked in that branch of them. I do not know what they are doing or how they are doing their docket.

DEFENCE LAWYER: Okay. Now, again my instructions are that when one comes from the scene the docket is brought to what is called a 24-hour inspection.

WITNESS: That is correct.

DEFENCE LAWYER: Did you bring the docket for a 24-hour inspection? Your docket.

WITNESS: As I have testified, I cannot recall what is contained in that docket because it is more than a year and that docket disappeared.

DEFENCE LAWYER: Okay, if you were to bring that docket for a 24-hour inspection, to whom were you supposed to bring the docket for such inspection?

WITNESS: To the commander.

DEFENCE LAWYER: And who was your commander?

WITNESS: The accused before Court.

DEFENCE LAWYER: Now, if he tells the Court, and he is going to do that, that you never brought that docket for the 24-hour inspection, what will you say?

WITNESS: I cannot comment on that because it was a long time ago.

DEFENCE LAWYER: So, you do not dispute that if he says that?

WITNESS: I cannot.

DEFENCE LAWYER: Who is the second in command to the accused at the office?

WITNESS: Captain Ngelese.

DEFENCE LAWYER: If Captain Ngelese is called and says the docket was never brought for 24-hour inspection, what would be your comment on that? Not even to him, as well as the commander.

WITNESS: I cannot recall.

DEFENCE LAWYER: So, it is one thing that you cannot dispute?

WITNESS: No.

DEFENCE LAWYER: Okay. Now, I am further instructed that it is procedure that, once the photos are taking from the scene, they are entered in what is called a photo register in your office?

WITNESS: That is correct.

DEFENCE LAWYER: Tell us when is it done? After how long is it done after the photos are taken from the scene?

WITNESS: I do not know because it is not the photographer; it is the admin personnel who made the entry.

DEFENCE LAWYER: Okay. Now, I am further instructed that according to the records currently available at your office, no photo register was ever entered in respect of the photos that you took.

WITNESS: As I have just testified now, it is part of the administrative personnel. They are the persons who are responsible for those entries.

DEFENCE LAWYER: But you must first submit the docket to administration, this is my instruction. It is my instruction again, Warrant Officer, that the registration of the photos is done when you have taken, as a photographer, the photos, and the work done on the scene to the commander and then from the commander within 24 hours it is then registered in the registers of the office.

WITNESS: It sounds right

DEFENCE LAWYER: Now, if you did – remember you do not recall whether you did bring it or not to the commander – if you did, any reason why it is not entered to date?

WITNESS: I cannot testify why another person is not doing their work.

DEFENCE LAWYER: This is what I am saying to you, Warrant Officer: you bring your work to the commander within 24 hours. He inspects your work and within 24 hours it is then registered in the photo register. Do you understand what I am saying?

WITNESS: Yes, that is right.

DEFENCE LAWYER: Do you agree with me on that?

WITNESS: Yes, that is correct.

DEFENCE LAWYER: Now, the question is: if you did bring it to the commander for the 24-hour inspection, why is it then not registered in the photo register until today?

WITNESS: I do not know.

DEFENCE LAWYER: I put it to you that you never took this docket for 24-hour inspection and you deliberately made it a point that it is not registered in the photo register.

WITNESS: That is not true.

DEFENCE LAWYER: Is it not your duty as a photographer to ensure that your work for the day has been registered in the register?

WITNESS: That is correct.

DEFENCE LAWYER: Have you done it up until this far? Have you ensured that?

WITNESS: My job was done well. If the docket was available I could tell you exactly what happened. The Court will also see the point that I want the Court to understand that there is no standing operating procedures to tell us what is going to happen to the docket.

COURT: When the suspect is the commander? So you are saying you do not know what the procedure is, or there is no procedure, where the suspect is a commanding officer? Is that what you saying?

WITNESS: What I am trying to say is, if I veer off the standard procedure it is because there is no standing operating procedure for me to do my work when the suspect is actually my commander.

DEFENCE LAWYER: So what you telling the Court now is that you might have breached those procedures for the reason that the suspect was the commander?

WITNESS: It is possible.

DEFENCE LAWYER: Okay, but there was a second in command, Captain Ngelese.

WITNESS: I go back to the fact that it was said that it must not become public knowledge.

DEFENCE LAWYER: Okay. So you were also keeping it secret from Captain Ngelese as well, up until today?

WITNESS: That is not true

DEFENCE LAWYER: Did you at any stage reveal it to Captain Ngelese? The case?

WITNESS: Yes, because I went to him on the 14th of March, according to this docket.

DEFENCE LAWYER: And if you did go to the Captain Ngelese, why was it not registered again?

WITNESS: You just said that until to date I kept it secret from Captain Ngelese and I said no.

DEFENCE LAWYER: Okay. Let us leave that point. Again, my instructions are that when a photographer is from the scene, the photos themselves are brought to the attention of the commander for what is called the quality inspection of those photos.

WITNESS: In the docket there is a diary. I cannot recall the time span.

DEFENCE LAWYER: That diary stipulates that when the photos are there, the commander must inspect it.

WITNESS: Say for argument sake, the time span is two weeks. Then, whether my docket is finalised in that period of 14 days... For argument's sake, what I am trying to say to Court is that when I have finished my album, then I can take my docket to the commander. He looks at the photos and he signs at the place and the key as well, and then he writes in the docket that he is happy with the content and the key of the photo album.

DEFENCE LAWYER: Thank you for your explanation. Do you agree that what I am saying is the procedure? Is that correct?

WITNESS: That is correct

DEFENCE LAWYER: Now, this is my question. Did you then take the photos for the quality inspection to the commander?

WITNESS: The album was handed to Captain Ngelese. I have already informed you that I cannot say what is contained in the docket because it disappeared.

DEFENCE LAWYER: To whom did you take the photos for inspection?

WITNESS: Captain Ngelese.

DEFENCE LAWYER: Thank you. You say when he has inspected the photos and assured that they are quality, he makes an entry to say he agrees with the quality?

WITNESS: Yes, there is a place there in the diary.

DEFENCE LAWYER: So, Captain Ngelese must have done it?

WITNESS: I do not know what Captain Ngelese did because I don't have my album and everything which was signed.

DEFENCE LAWYER: Let me just inform you. I do not want you to comment on this. We are going to call Captain Ngelese to testify. Now, I am further instructed when a senior officer is involved in any case it is procedure that another senior duty officer is called to the scene. Do you agree with that?

WITNESS: It sounds right.

DEFENCE LAWYER: What is that? Your question is whether you agree or not?

WITNESS: You are asking me something which is out of my duties, so I cannot give you a definite answer. At no stage do I have to call a senior personnel. That is the duty of the investigating officer.

DEFENCE LAWYER: Again, I thank you for the good lengthy explanation. My question is, do you agree with that?

WITNESS: You asked me why I answered my question and then I verified it.

DEFENCE LAWYER: Do you want to answer my question, Warrant Officer?

WITNESS: Then ask it again.

DEFENCE LAWYER: Now, if it sounds right then it is in accordance with my instructions. When you visited the scene together with Lesley there was no senior officer at all?

WITNESS: That question is supposed to be asked to Warrant Officer Lesley.

DEFENCE LAWYER: I ask if from you because you were also at the scene.

WITNESS: The only time that we can ask a senior as well to come to the scene is when a senior crime has been committed.

DEFENCE LAWYER: Yes, I am still going to that. Let us deal with my question first. When you were at the scene with Warrant Officer Lesley, there was no senior officer?

WITNESS: That is correct.

DEFENCE LAWYER: Do you consider fraud as a less serious crime?

WITNESS: On that day, fraud was not the charge of the case on that day.

DEFENCE LAWYER: Do you get my question?

WITNESS: That is why I answered it.

DEFENCE LAWYER: No, you have not answered it. My question is, do you consider fraud as a less serious crime?

WITNESS: You asked me, do I consider it less and I said I do not. So I do consider it serious.

DEFENCE LAWYER: Warrant Officer, have you ever been convicted of fraud?

WITNESS: I was.

DEFENCE LAWYER: Now, I am advised that the reason you always had an axe to grind against the accused is that when you were applying for a promotion sometime in 2009, you dishonestly wrote on the form meant for that purpose that you do not have previous conviction.

WITNESS: That is incorrect. Am I allowed to continue further?

DEFENCE LAWYER: But even at the stage when you submitted your application to the accused, he told you that he must first verify the truthfulness of whether you do have a previous conviction or not.

WITNESS: No, that is not true.

DEFENCE LAWYER: Now, when you were applying for a senior rank from inspector, is it correct that you were shortlisted?

WITNESS: That is correct

DEFENCE LAWYER: Who then signed your form that is supposed to be signed by the commander?

WITNESS: I cannot recall because it was 2009.

DEFENCE LAWYER: My instructions are that, for the reason that the accused queried that you have a previous conviction, you quarrelled with him and in fact your form was sent somewhere else. Hence you were shortlisted.

WITNESS: It is the first time that I hear that. I cannot recall any quarrel on any previous convictions.

DEFENCE LAWYER: You do not recall yourself quarrelling with the accused for (inaudible)?

WITNESS: That is just what I was testifying to.

DEFENCE LAWYER: Okay. Now. Just tell us – this one is very simple – I am instructed that in your office when you need accident reconstruction experts you obtain them from Pretoria. Is that correct?

DEFENCE LAWYER: My last question yesterday was, are you sure there are no experts?

WITNESS: Yes it is. There are no experts.

DEFENCE LAWYER: Okay. And you are not experts as well?

WITNESS: Yes, it is.

DEFENCE LAWYER: Specifically, is there an accident reconstruction expert in your office?

WITNESS: No.

DEFENCE LAWYER: Do you know Warrant Officer van Onselen?

WITNESS: Yes, I do.

DEFENCE LAWYER: He is also part of your office?

WITNESS: Yes, he is.

DEFENCE LAWYER: And you have known him for some time?

WITNESS: Yes it is, Your Worship.

DEFENCE LAWYER: Are you then saying that even himself is not an expert?

WITNESS: Yes it is, Your Worship

DEFENCE LAWYER: He is not an expert, a reconstruction expert, either?

WITNESS: He only has knowledge, Your Worship. He is not an expert.

DEFENCE LAWYER: I am asking this because he told the Court under oath that he is an expert.

WITNESS: He is a fingerprint expert, Your Worship.

DEFENCE LAWYER: And he is not an accident reconstruction expert at all?

WITNESS: Yes, it is, Your Worship.

DEFENCE LAWYER: Now let me – I apologise for this, Your Worship, for going back a little bit – there was an issue about the quality assurance that you say was signed by Captain Ngelese?

WITNESS: I never said he signed the quality assurance. The only thing I said is that he signed my album.

DEFENCE LAWYER: What does it mean? Does it mean he was assuring the quality of the photos in the album?

WITNESS: No, that is not what I am saying. Wat ek se is dat die album geteken is, maar ek kan nie testify op die quality signature nie, omdat die docket nie daar is nie.

INTERPRETER: The docket was not there, but the album was signed. I do not know if it was the quality that he signed

DEFENCE LAWYER: So, as you are standing here now, you cannot tell the Court if the photos were certified as of good quality as it is supposed to be?

WITNESS: I do not have the docket.

DEFENCE LAWYER: Yes, exactly, and you cannot tell the Court that those photos were certified as of good quality? You cannot say that?

WITNESS: Yes, it is, Your Worship.

DEFENCE LAWYER: Now, when did you bring these things for signature by Captain Ngelese?

WITNESS: You can check on the docket, Your Worship, on the date when the statement was made

DEFENCE LAWYER: You cannot estimate as to when?

WITNESS: No.

DEFENCE LAWYER: Now let us move further. Are you also a forensic investigator?

WITNESS: Yes, it is.

DEFENCE LAWYER: Okay, Now in your training are you also trained in the keeping of exhibits that are taken from the scene?

WITNESS: Yes, it is so.

DEFENCE LAWYER: It is where all the offences should start, before they can go to DPP and even go to Court. Do you agree with that?

WITNESS: Yes.

DEFENCE LAWYER: Now, in this particular case in the criminal record system of the police there is no charge of fraud against the accused. Do you agree with that?

WITNESS: The document that I have just been handed in Court, I do not know where that document comes from. I do not work in that section that draws those documents. I cannot comment on it.

DEFENCE LAWYER: I am putting to you that there is no such charge next to his name.

WITNESS: Okay, and then?

DEFENCE LAWYER: Do you agree with me that and the document reflects that?

WITNESS: You say so. I do not know that document. I do not know where it was obtained from. I do know the procedures when obtaining it, whether it would be correct. I cannot testify about that.

DEFENCE LAWYER: It is so that, if does not appear in the criminal record system, it means something went wrong and the whole case jumped the level of the police to the DPP when the decision was made.

WITNESS: I do not know those procedures. I cannot testify to that.

DEFENCE LAWYER: Okay, it might be an administrative error. Lastly, I am instructed again, and you may comment on this if you like, that this whole fraud thing is a conspiracy between yourself and Warrant Officer Lesley against your commander, the accused.

WITNESS: As I have testified yesterday, Your Worship, that is not the truth.

DEFENCE LAWYER: Your Worship, just an instruction. I am further instructed that when the current commander, the accused before Court, arrived at your branch office, you and other investigators, including Warrant Officer Lesley, used to sit there in the offices doing nothing and he chased them away and you were angry about it. The reason for chasing is that no police officials are allowed, in fact it is policy, only person working there are allowed,

WITNESS: That is not the truth.

DEFENCE LAWYER: I am further instructed that you never accepted him as your commander.

WITNESS: That is not the truth as well

DEFENCE LAWYER: And that at all times you undermine him and report straight to the province and not to him, because you were not accepting the commander.

WITNESS: That is not the truth.

DEFENCE LAWYER: No further questions, Your Worship. Thank you.

COURT ASKING QUESTIONS

COURT: You can answer this question if you know. If you can tell me the answer. What is the procedure when there is an investigation against a senior officer in the police? How is that supposed to go about? Is it supposed to be investigated by the same people in the area or does somebody else from outside have to come in and investigate?

WITNESS: The only thing I know, Your Worship, about internal, I do not know if the person is on the same level or a higher rank. I am not sure how does it happen.

COURT: You are excused, Sir.

WITNESS: Thank You, Your Worship.

PROSECUTOR: The State is then closing is case

END OF THE STATE CASE

CHAPTER TWELVE

APPLICATION FOR DISCHARGE IN TERMS OF SECTION 174

DEFENCE LAWYER: Your Worship, at this stage my instruction is to move for an application in terms of Section 174 of the Criminal Procedure Act. It is my submission, Your Worship, that on the evidence presented before the Court up until this stage no reasonable Court can find against the accused, convict him.

COURT: Response from the State? Are you still busy? Sorry, yes, carry on.

DEFENCE LAWYER: Your Worship, at this stage the Court is expected to consider the evidence presented by the State and make a finding whether that evidence will stand alone. The Court will be able to convict the accused. Various cases have been reported on that.

The case of *S vs Van Wyk* comes to mind and the Court at this stage is expected to look at that evidence. I am sorry if... I am sorry if I am repeating this. Very strange things have happened in this matter. Your Worship, it is common cause that the Court is always the last level of the criminal justice system. It begins with the police and when it begins, the accused is given his fundamental rights of having a say to a charge that is preferred against him. They call it a warning statement. That is the basic right.

Now, in this particular case that was not done. Now, in effect, before Your Worship you are having an accused who has been wrongfully brought before the Court in serious breach of fundamental rights. It means the very person who decided that this matter must be prosecuted and dealt with in this Court heard no version of the accused at all. That is a very serious breach of fundamental and constitutional right of the accused. Now to sum up that point before you, is a person wrongly brought before you and it is my submission that this Court should not be part of what is clearly unlawful.

This Court cannot deal with this matter. In fact, should not have dealt with this matter had it been known that such a serious fundamental breach of his constitutional right was made. That is the first point, and at this stage the Court should discharge the accused solely on the basis of that. He is wrongly before you.

Your Worship, the second point. The accused is charged with fraud. I do not need to repeat the elements of fraud. They are well known. Now, from the evidence of what I consider to be the crucial and the main witness, the investigator, we are now made aware that no docket was opened for a fraud case at all. That is on record. Perhaps it again goes to the breach of the fundamental rights of the accused. Now, the question is, how did it happen that the accused is appearing before you without any docket?

Of much importance, Warrant Officer Lesley tells the Court in no uncertain terms that whatever was done by him in investigating the case or the information or the allegation about the collision at the Bedford road brought no prejudice at all to him as an investigator and according to him nobody was prejudiced by that. It is his duty, normal routine, to follow every link of information and according to him he has brought no prejudice at all to anybody

COURT: Well, fraud also involves potential prejudice and not just prejudice per say.

DEFENCE LAWYER: I am talking about what the witness had said.

COURT: But the elements are not just prejudice. It is potential prejudice.

DEFENCE LAWYER: But I am still addressing prejudice.

COURT: I know.

DEFENCE LAWYER: Now there is an issue, let me just deal with that, of potential prejudice which point on the evidence had been brought before Court so that the Court is aware what potential prejudice could have been there as the result allegedly or the accused had pointed a difference scene to where the collision has taken place.

COURT: I am not in agreement with the argument there, and I will explain to you in my judgment.

DEFENCE LAWYER: The point I am making, Your Worship, is that evidence should be led in that regard and the Court from the evidence is going to make a finding that...

COURT: Yes, and I will give my reasoning in my judgment.

DEFENCE LAWYER: Now, Your Worship, from the evidence of Warrant Officer Lesley there is no... rather, let me put it this way.. up until this stage, when the State has closed, there is no evidence at all from the source of information. The Court will be reminded that all the witnesses that testified, they do not have the first-hand information as to what happened at the Bedford road.

Warrant Officer Lesley told the Court that he himself was informed by a person whom he refused to disclose his name in this Court. Now, the status of that evidence is nothing else,

I submit, but hearsay evidence that remains unconfirmed until the end of the State case. He was only told the name was not disclosed and that person unfortunately has not been called up until now. Now, the Court is only left with inadmissible type of evidence up to now.

Now, on those versions, Your Worship, it is my submission that there is no need, with respect, to call the accused to answer to what is not admissible before Court, being the hearsay.

The Court can at this stage discharge the accused on the basis of no evidence as it were.

Now, let me quickly rush to the second witness that I consider to be crucial as well. The last witness, Warrant Officer De Klerk. The sole reason for him being called to testify was for him to testify about the role that he made at the Bedford road and, Your Worship, it is my submission that the quality of the evidence that he brought before Court leaves much to be desired.

It is clear from his evidence that all the procedures were flouted. Your Worship, it is my submission that the Court cannot consider that evidence as it were. It is evidence that deserves nothing but to be thrown out of the window, with respect.

Now there is evidence that I must touch on quickly without wasting time. The evidence of Warrant Officer van Onselen. He told the Court that he is an expert. Today we are told that he was not telling the truth. He gave evidence only when asked by the Court to say his opinion as an expert and observations were in fact that the accident did not take place on the N2 road, but Your Worship when he was asked as to why he did not mention this as far back as the 1st of March 2010, there was absolutely no explanation. He concealed this information even to my learned friend.

Your Worship, the only inference that can be drawn, and that is the only one, is that what he was saying before Court was nothing but an afterthought that cannot be admitted and accepted. For the simple reason that it denied the accused throughout to prepare for that type of evidence and even to deal with it. It comes when he was giving evidence. Only when he was asked by the Court. He did not give that evidence at all. Your Worship, without wasting this Court's time, I have made my point and I believe strongly, Your Worship, that there is no case (inaudible). The Court should find with respect (inaudible)

COURT: That is fine. Submissions from the State?

PROSECUTOR: I will leave it in the hands of the Court

CHAPTER THIRTEEN

JUDGMENT OF THE COURT

AT THE STAGE OF THE proceedings, the Court is called upon to decide whether or not in the case of the case before the Court, the Court is of the opinion that if there is no evidence that the accused committed the offence referred to in the charge it may return a verdict of not guilty. At the outset, it is clear that in this case we are not dealing with a normal criminal investigation. The allegations against the accused were initially started as that of reckless and negligent driving and it is also clear that the accused is also a senior member in the South African Police Service.

I am in disagreement with the Defence in connection with the warning statement. It is clear that the matter was opened as a case of reckless and negligent driving. Especially, the matter of no docket in the fraud case. I am also in disagreement with Defence regarding the fact of prejudice, because it is clear there was a fraud case against the accused that was opened. The allegations against the accused are clear, as according to the charge sheet. The problem, however, arises in the manner in which the case was investigated. Clearly, being a senior member in the Local Criminal Record Centre, this matter should not have been handled by anybody in that office.

Also, clearly procedures were not followed, but there is no evidence before the Court on the State's side as to what should have happened in a case like this. The Court can therefore not rely on the evidence of the police officers who testified from the Local Criminal Record Centre.

Obviously, the other problem that the State has today is the fact that they have handed in a Section 212 statement which has no weight. Now, the Court cannot make any evidence credibility finding against Mr Lesley because his evidence was clear to the Court. Given the nature of the allegations and the fact the accused is a senior officer in the South African Police Service, the Court can understand why certain information was dealt with in the way that is what dealt with but, as the Court has pointed out, it should not have been dealt with by anybody in the vicinity of Grahamstown, if they seriously wanted to investigate this matter objectively.

Having said so, the Court has had to actually meander its way mindful of issues that are not really relevant to the issue at hand. The issue is whether there is any evidence before the Court upon which a Court at this stage can convict the accused. The State has not placed any reliable information before the Court which would actually call for the accused to answer in the case. Therefore, the accused will have to be given the benefit of the doubt and is found not guilty.

***

On the day I was found not guilty in terms of Section 174 of the Criminal Procedure Act, 1977, I released a statement to the media in an effort to inform the people of Grahamstown and Eastern Cape that the so-called fraud levelled against was a false case and non-existent from the beginning

Top cop vows to blow lid off alleged corruption

KWANELE BUTANA

A SENIOR policeman acquitted of fraud charges this week now says he's going to spill the beans on alleged corruption and racism in the unit of which he's in charge.

This week the Grahamstown Magistrate's Court found Lt Colonel Tengimpilo Maqebhula not guilty of fraud and said the state had presented no evidence that supported the charge levelled against him.

Appearing before Magistrate Nishani Beharie on Wednesday, Maqebhula was represented by Mthatha-based attorney Vuyani Msindo and the state prosecutor was Mandisi Gwatyuza.

It was alleged in the fraud charges against Maqebhula that in February last year, he signed out a police vehicle to drive from Grahamstown to Port Elizabeth for work purposes. Later that day, the car had been involved in an accident – not on the N2, however, but on the R350 between Grahamstown and Bedford. Maqebhula had allegedly reported that he'd hit a kudu on his way to Port Elizabeth.

At first, Maqebhula had faced internal charges of statutory reckless and negligent driving.

However, parts of the Fiat Siena he had been driving, animal intestines and blood stains were allegedly found on the R350 three days later,

RETURN TO INNOCENCE... Grahamstown commander of the Criminal Record Centre Lt Colonel Tengimpilo Maqebhula (right) shares a joke with his lawyer Vuyani Msindo as they leave the Grahamstown Magistrate's Court after his acquittal on Wednesday. He had been charged with fraud. Photo: Supplied

and a fraud case was opened against him.

Delivering her judgment, Beharie questioned the fact that investigations against a high-ranking officer had been carried out by his subordinates from within Grahamstown.

Beharie said if the police had been serious about the investigations against Maqebhula, a senior officer from outside the area should have investigated the matter. Therefore she could not accept the evidence presented to her by the state.

The fraud case has been complicated by allegations of racism in the Eastern Cape provincial police department, with Maqebhula saying that what he described as a blanket of racism covering the police Criminal Record Centre was backed by senior officers in the province.

Maqebhula believes he was targeted as a result of questions he had been asking about the Criminal Record Centre since he was appointed its commander in 2009.

Promoted from the Cradock Criminal Record Centre in 2009, Maqebhula told Grocott's Mail that when he arrived at the Grahamstown office, he discovered that one of the employees in his centre had a criminal record that included convictions for theft, forgery and fraud.

These crimes had not been reported to the South African Police Service Criminal Bureau, however, contrary to the provisions of the Criminal Procedure Act of 1977.

Maqebhula said he had reported the matter to the provincial Criminal Record Centre management, telling them that in terms of Criminal Bureau ethics, the department could not retain someone convicted of a crime. They brushed him off, he said, accusing him of being "too personal".

Visibly relieved at his acquittal, Maqebhula said in an emotionally charged interview with Grocott's Mail outside the court, "The truth has finally come out. I never committed fraud, or [even] any less serious offence throughout my career.

"It's not a mistake that a black colonel was appointed to head this centre. I am not apologetic about being black," Maqebhula said, alleging that his subordinates tried to order him around because they were white.

"One thing I will never do is to take orders from my juniors".

Maqebhula said he knew black police officers who had been dismissed from their jobs for charges which emanated from racism in the department. He alleged that criminal records of white police officers did not get registered in the national Criminal Record System.

"Enough is enough, I will spill the beans to the end," he said.

I believed that I, and many black and coloured police officers, were not treated equally before the law. The belief was informed by many cases that were opened against white police officers, where the same white prosecutors were the first people to know and they always gave pressure to investigating officers to bring docket for decision. Those investigators were given a pressure to submit an empty docket for decision, and all declined to prosecute.

But many black and coloured police officers, like myself, were prosecuted but were found not guilty in terms of Section 174 of the Criminal Procedure Act, 1977. At the same, time the following former South African Police Service members were charged and found not guilty in terms of section 174, but were already dismissed departmentally: late former Sergeant Mthana; former Constable Nabo, Mame, and Sergeant Hoza.

After my case, coloured former Sergeants Sauls, Prince, Brown, Constable Freeman and many more were also dismissed and are now suing the state for unlawful arrest and malicious prosecution.

I therefore wrote a detailed letter to the South African Human Rights Commission and to the National Director of Public Prosecutions requesting answers as to how I could be in court for a false case, which did not even have complainant, and was never reported at Grahamstown police station. I got responses that matters would be investigated but nothing happened.

Corporate Services

ITIONAL PROSECUTING AUTHORITY
South Africa

Ref:	IMU 550 02/01/13
Enq:	Sejeng D
Tel:	012 845 6661

TO: **Lt. Col. T. Maqebhula**
South African Police Service
Office of the Commander
Grahamstown

FROM: **Ms. D. Sejeng**
Senior Special Investigator: IMU

DATE: 11 February 2013

SUBJECT: **ACKNOWLEDGEMENT OF A COMPLAINT**

During the month of January 2013, the Integrity Management Unit (herein referred to as IMU) in NPA received a complaint regarding maladministration, corrupt activities and racism in Grahamstown. It is alledged that there is a cruel relationship between white NPA prosecutors and white SAPS officials in Grahamstown whilst executing their duties.

It was reported that each case which is opened against a white policeman in Grahamstown, Cradock, Graaf Reinet and all other areas around Grahamstown is known by white NPA prosecutors and the investigator will be given pressure to bring the docket and it will be declined for prosecution.

The complaint has been registered as IMU 550 02/01/13 and the investigator on the matter is Ms D Sejeng

Kind regards,

MS D. SEJENG
SENIOR SPECIAL INVESTIGATROR: IMU
NATIONAL PROSECUTING AUTHORITY (NPA)
DATE:

SOUTH AFRICAN HUMAN RIGHTS COMMISSION

4th Floor Oxford House
86-88 Oxford Street
East London
5200

P.O. Box 972
East London
5200

Tel: (043) 7227828/21/25
Fax: (043) 7227830
e-mail: lmpondo@sahrc.org.za

Mr Tengimpilo Maqebhula
Criminal Record & Crime Scene Management
SAPS
GRAHAMSTOWN

Our Ref: EC/2011/0260/NT

Date: 05 September 2011

By fax: 046 603 9327

Dear Sir

YOUR COMPLAINT

The above matter refers.

The South African Human Rights Commission has been established to investigate the violations of human rights as contained in the Bill of Rights, which is Chapter 2 of the Constitution.

The Commission is empowered by its Regulations to refer some of its complaints to other bodies or organisations that can deal with the said dispute most effectively and expeditiously than the Commission.

Kindly take note that your complaint has been referred to the office of the Provincial Commissioner for assistance, hence the matter falls within their ambits.

We will keep you abreast with any further developments herein.

Yours faithfully

Adv. LE Mpondo
PO Acting Provincial Manager

As I'd already sent letters to the Police management and Human Rights commission long before I was taken to court and charged, I released a detailed statement in an effort to appeal for help against the abuse of power and perceived racism in the police.

Saturday Dispatch, October 8, 2011

Black SAPS members cry racism

By **BONGANI FUZILE**
Crime Reporter

THE SOUTH African Police Service (SAPS) in the Eastern Cape has been rocked by allegations of racism, with white members accused of discriminating against black colleagues.

Police members from Grahamstown police station have written a letter of complaint to the Human Rights Commission (HRC).

They said their complaints about racism to their employer and to various police ministers had fallen on deaf ears.

In the letter to the HRC, it was claimed that some black and coloured members were dismissed from work for crimes they never committed while their white colleagues, who committed similar offences, received suspended sentences or were never prosecuted at all.

The author of the letter to the HRC, Lieutenant Colonel Tengimpilo Maqebhula, who is the coordinator of the Racism Victims group, said SAPS members were fed up with what was happening.

He said similar issues had arisen at Cradock police station and at the Criminal Records Centre (CRC) at police headquarters in King William's Town.

"Racial tension has reached boiling point (and) could explode at any time. Racism is rife within the SAPS and we've been to many offices including those of ministers to try to get help but nothing happened, hence we've approached the HRC," said Maqebhula.

HRC to intervene urgently.

In the letter, he said black commanders were leaving the CRC unit as they could not tolerate racism.

"Black commanders don't see their value at (the CRC) and other units as they are undermined by their white juniors," he said.

He also referred to cases where black members were dismissed despite never being convicted of the criminal charges they had faced.

These were:

● In 2000, a police constable was accused of rape. Charges against him were dropped but he was discharged from work; and

● A case of stock theft was brought against a police sergeant in the same year. He was later released by the courts but he was also discharged from the police.

He compared these to cases involving white members:

● In 1997 a white member stole cheques from a crime scene. He was charged for the crimes and received a suspended sentence. He is still employed by the SAPS; and

● In 2008 a Cradock police member was charged for stealing fuel using a State petrol card but his case was "manipulated", despite having a number of witnesses. He is still employed by SAPS.

Another member of the Racism Victims group, David Mthana, said a black person had no say in the police. "Racism is still there. I lost my job because I was accused of theft. I was later acquitted but I lost my job," said Mthana.

HRC national spokesman Vincent Moaga confirmed receipt of the complaint from Maqebhula. "We've written to the Grahamstown police to get a response to these allegations."

Police, Prisons and Civil Rights Union (Popcru) Eastern Cape deputy provincial secretary Zamikhaya Skade said there were isolated cases of racism. "We've got cases in Queenstown and Graaff-Reinet and there's a joint team working on that," said Skade. — *bonganif@dispatch.co.za*

CHAPTER FOURTEEN

Interview with former Sergeant Mthana, who was dismissed

AFTER RELEASING THE STATEMENT IN the Daily Dispatch on the 8th of August 2011, I noticed comments by someone of the name of David Mthana, who was actually saying that he had been dismissed by the South African Police Service for a crime never committed and further that racism is still the order of the day in Grahamstown Police.

He later visited me and I interviewed him. He told me that the Human Resource section of the Police is always managed by white police and it is them who decide who must be dismissed and who must be covered up. He further told me that a false case will be created by white police and presented to the Deputy Director of Public Prosecution office, to the same white prosecutors and state advocates in Grahamstown.

A minute saying that you must be prosecuted will be issued. Once that minute is issued, you will be quickly subjected to a disciplinary hearing and at that stage you are already dismissed. The hearings were always conducted by white police only. He further told me that he was taken to Port Elizabeth to a place called Noma House and was simply dismissed. When he arrived in Port Elizabeth, he was informed by a black lady, who was a cleaner, that black police are all dismissed, for going there is just a formality and sanction of dismissal is already drafted.

He also gave me the already drafted statement as follows:

> I worked under the oppression by white police members of Grahamstown since 1990 as a detective and was

working for the Narcotic Branch. During 1999, I arrested a white male at Bathusrt, who was dealing in liquor without a licence, and that person told me he needed a white police officer, not a black police member, to arrest him.

After the white police in Grahamstown noticed that I had arrested a white person they became furious and I was harassed and transferred to Springs, Johannesburg, Detective Branch. I later managed to come back to my family.

While I was on duty in Grahamstown, I was travelling with a white police officer and that white police officer requested me to help him to get a sheep on a farm. I was driving but on the way I noticed some other white policeman and they stopped us and I was arrested and that police officer was not arrested. I was quickly subjected to a disciplinary hearing and was dismissed.

The regional court magistrate who found me not guilty in terms Section 174 of the Criminal procedure Act, 1977, mentioned in his judgement that it was a dirty game played by the police.

At the same time, a white police officer was arrested for stealing a cheque of about R1 300 and cashing it in Port Elizabeth. He was arrested and charged for theft and fraud and he pleaded guilty and was found guilty and fined R200. At the departmental hearing, he was fined R500 and was still working for South African Police Service.

Furthermore, a police captain was charged for assault with GBH and was found guilty for assaulting his colleague and his girlfriend, but was given a warning at the departmental hearing and allowed to go back to work.

He also informed me that he had reported all these unlawful actions to the police management, but nothing happened. He later reported to the office of the Minister of Police and he showed me the response, but nothing happened, except a response that the matters would be investigated. He also furnished me with the written recommendation by his station commander of Grahamstown, Colonel Kol, while the white police were pushing for suspension as follows:

LETTER From the MEC FOR SAFETY AND SECURITY

Iphondo Lwempuma-koloni   Province of the Eastern Cape   Provinsie Oos-Kaap

| ISEBE LOKHUSELO NOKHUSELEKO | DEPARTMENT OF SAFETY AND SECURITY | DEPARTEMENT VAN VEILIGHEID EN SEKURITEIT |

Ingxowa Eyodwa/Private Bag/Privaatsak X0057, BISHO 5605, SOUTH AFRICA

Ireferensi
Ref. No.   10/6/1
Varwysings Nr

Imibuzo   **NEIL NAIDOO**
Enquiries
Navrac

Ifoni
Telephone 040-6092749
Telefoon

Ifaxi   040-6391320
Facsimile
Faksimilee

08 February 2000

A.   The Provincial Commissioner
     Attention Commissioner Noqayi
     Fax 041-3946650

B.   The Area Commissioner - Grahamstown
     Attention Director Toba
     Fax 046-6039123

C.   Office of the Area Commissioner - Grahamstown
     Attention Sgt Mthana
     Fax 046-6039202

**SUBJECT : GRIEVANCE AND ALLEGED RACISM AGAINST SGT. MTHANA
NO: 0174056-3**

A+B1. By direction of the MEC for Safety, Liaison and Transport Mr Dennis Neer I am referring the above matter to your offices for urgent attention

2.   We would also request a thorough investigation as to why the said members salary should not immediately be reinstated as he has already been acquitted and discharged of the alleged false case against him.

3.   Our offices are concerned about the numerous complaints we are getting regarding the alleged racism against black members from the disciplinary trial officers.

4.   We are further requesting that the background to the incident whereby the complainant alleges that white members of the stock theft unit set a trap for him also be investigated taking into consideration that the complainant was acquited.

5.   The alleged statement by Inspector Botha in (para. 9) must also be investigated as continuously we are informed that black members are discharged by white trial officers before they appear at their disciplinary hearing.

6.   The MEC, Mr D. Neer view these allegations as serious and request that this matter receives urgent and priority attention.

7.   We would appreciate a written response within three (3) days, and would request that this member's salary immediately be reinstated.

8.   I thank you for your co-operation

Regards

NEIL NAIDOO
DEPUTY DIRECTOR MONITORING : EASTERN CAPE

Sgt. Mthana - Copy for your information

4.   <u>In favour of the accused</u> :

4.1   According to the statements Police received information of the
      alleged stocktheft well in advance. Due to inexplicable reasons the
      person was not arrested on the scene of the crime. Why not? What is
      then the purpose of observation, with no action! Sergeant Mthana was
      according to the statements seen throwing the sheep over a wall.
      Logically he must have stopped the police vehicle, got out and got
      rid of the sheep. If he was seen, why wasn't he arrested on the
      scene of the crime?

4.2   What happened to the three other suspects. The police had a perfect
      opportunity to arrest them all with Sergeant Mthana on the scene of
      the crime. This did not materialize. Why not? Now the other three
      suspects are at large and the police seems not to know their
      identity.

4.3   Why wasn't the correct procedures followed with the exhibits? Why
      could the jersey (exhibit), not be sealed in the presence of the
      accused or placed in the exhibit safe which is meant for this
      purpose. Surely there can be doubts?

5.   RECOMMENDATION :

5.1   There are too many why's for which there are no immediate answers.

5.2   The police initially had a very good case, but due to inexplicable
      reasons did not live up to its expectations in terms of
      professionalism and arresting of the suspects on the scene.

      This could have proved the case beyond reasonable doubt. Now there
      are doubts which just cannot be ignored.

6.   Suspension is not recommended in terms of paragraph 4..1, 4.2 and
      4.3 and it is suggested that the member work under supervision and
      his driving authority be withdrawn.

................................S/SUPERINTENDENT
STATION COMMISSIONER : GRAHAMSTOWN
(R S KOLL)

me/lib00

CHAPTER FIFTEEN

Interview of former Constable Mame

ANOTHER VICTIM, FORMER CONSTABLE XOLANI Mame, came and told me that, in the same period of David Mthana's dismissal, he was subjected to a disciplinary hearing as a result of a rape case opened by his girlfriend. He was taken to Noma House in Port Elizabeth and spotted that a judgement of dismissal had already been written. He told me the same story as former Seargeant Mthana, that you will be quickly hauled to disciplinary hearing.

He informed me further that he was found not guilty in the criminal case and former Constable Nabo was his defence witness and Nabo was quickly charged for attempted murder and taken to a disciplinary hearing and dismissed and the criminal case was then simply withdrawn.

As former Constable Mame was found not guilty on rape, the matter was well publicised in the paper, the Daily Dispatch, and reads as follows:

> Suspended local policeman Xolani Mame, 30, shed tears of relief when he was acquitted of a rape charge in the Grahamstown Regional Court yesterday. Mame was accused of raping Thandiswa Maphipha (26) at the Makanaskop Police station in January last year. Magistrate Dunywa said, "The State's case was full of improbabilities and the same could not be said of the defence".
> Dunywa further said it was impossible that Maphaphu went to Mame's room in the police barracks just to pick up a video cassette after thrice rejecting his love proposals. He rejected Maphaphu's testimony that she did not want

to lay charges at the Makanaskop police station because she feared her case would not be believed.

He said it was also clear that Maphaphu would not have laid charges were it not for the assistance of her aunt Xolaswa Nika. The medical report showed no clinical evidence of rape and there was no evidence that Maphaphu's clothes had been torn. He said it was clear that the only thing that led to a rape charge being laid was Mame's failure to give Maphaphu the taxi fare he'd promised to give her.

Magistrate Dunywa said Mame's version of consensual sex was corroborated by Constable Daliwanga Nabo, who said that he had not heard any scream as Maphaphu had testified. Nabo and Mame's rooms were close to his office and he would have heard Maphaphu scream.

Former Constable Nabo told me that an attempted murder case was opened and withdrawn. It was just a plan to get rid of him because he testified in Mame's case.

Ten years later, the following police were dismissed by the police department in Grahamstown, for allegations in cases they never committed: former Seargeants Hoza and Guwa, former Constable Booi, late former Constable Fiyani, AND coloured Sergeants Sauls, Prince, Brown and Hoffman. They were all in court found not guilty in terms Section 174 of the Criminal Procedure Act,1977, like myself and former late Sergeant Mthana and many more black and coloured police who were dismissed.

I talked to them one by one, starting with former Sergeant Hoza. He told me that he was involved in an accident with a state vehicle in 2016 and a criminal case was withdrawn but he was quickly subjected to a disciplinary case and the chairperson was a white police officer. He was already informed that he was going to be dismissed, like all other black police officers who were dismissed. He further informed me that reckless and negligent driving, especially if no person was injured, is a minor case compared with a case of Constable Zeeli (white police officer) who was charged for allowing a prisoner to escape but was simply given a one month salary suspension on departmental case no 58/2018 and is still working in the police force.

CHAPTER SIXTEEN

Interview with former Sergeant Sauls and Constable Freeman

FORMER SERGEANT SAULS AND FORMER Constable Freeman visited me and I interviewed them and they told me that they were arrested and detained on charges of theft of liquor, in that during the month of October 2019 a truck of Southern African Breweries was involved in an accident and allegedly they took beer and loaded it into the police van and, instead of handing it back to the owner, they took it to Mandisa Tarven and sold it.

The theft case was registered as Joza Cas 56/11/2020, and they were released on bail. They further told me that they were quickly subjected to a disciplinary hearing under case no 269/11/2020 and charged in terms of the new SAPS disciplinary regulations as follows: Regulation 5(3) (a), 5(3) (i), 5(3) (u), in that you failed perform any act with the intention to under the policy of the South Africa Police service by stealing a case of beer and Regulation 5(3) (t)), conducted himself in an improper, disgracefully and unacceptable manner in that you and constable, in that you steal a case of beer.

They further told me that, at the disciplinary hearing, they were never afforded their constitutional rights, particularly Section 35(5) (i) of the Constitution that says every accused person has a right to adduce and challenge evidence presented against him or her and to cross question witnesses. They further informed me that the South African Police Disciplinary Regulations were amended to have two procedures.

The first is the normal disciplinary process that is provided for in terms Labour Regulations Act of 1995 and that procedure is practised by all employers in the Republic of South Africa.

The second procedure is called the Expeditious Process and is outlined in Regulation 9 and they described it as unconstitutional. How it works is that firstly there are list of offences that qualify to be subjected to this process. To mention but a few, fraud, theft, housebreaking, rape, escaping of a prisoner from lawful custody, negligent loss of fire arm, assault with grievous bodily harm, sexual harassment and others.

If there are allegations that you committed these departmental offences, an investigation is conducted quickly and you will be summoned to appear before the chairperson who is at the level of a brigadier or above. This brigadier will simply read charges and quote statement witnesses and ask whether you agree with the witness statements and charges.

Whether you agree or disagree, that brigadier is empowered by these Regulations to pronounce a sanction without calling witnesses to testify and giving a chance to cross examine them, as provided for in terms of Section 35 (5) of the Constitution.

And you will be dismissed and there is no appeal. You have to take the matter to Safety Security and Sectorial Bargaining Chamber of the South African Police Service (SSSBC).

They told me that they were subjected to that process and were dismissed without being given a chance to cross examine witness. In short, they were dismissed with evidence based on hearsay evidence. They further told me that, although South African Police Regulations were unconstitutional, some white police officers who have a history of transplanting or manufacturing false cases against black and coloured police officers, hijacked this unconstitutional process and subjected all black and coloured police and used this process to dismiss them. They have not subjected white police officers, even if they committed offences listed as part of the expeditious process.

They made mention of a white female captain who called black police officers in the parade at Joza Police station, Grahamstown, monkeys. Such a charge of discrimination or racism falls under the category of expeditious process, but she was never subjected to the expeditious process. However, former Sergeant Brown, a coloured police officer, charged with assault common and breaking Covid-19 Regulations, was subjected to expeditious process and was dismissed, although these two charges belong to normal disciplinary regulations. In court, the case was simply withdrawn.

They further mentioned that another white male captain was charged with sexual harassment, which falls under the category of Regulation 9 expeditious process, but was never subjected to expeditious process.

They also revealed that white police officers are the most privileged and they are protected. They made mention of a white female captain working in the same station in Grahamstown, who negligently left her firearm in the office drawer. Mzwandile Magacu, who was a police informer, took the firearm and committed murder and robbery that same day in Grahamstown, and was sentenced to 20 years in Grahamstown case 214/06/1996. No steps were taken against that captain and she is still working in the police.

Former Sergeant Sauls told me that the justice system in Grahamstown NPA offices have eyes and ears and he gave an example of Grahamstown cas 116/06/2015, Hit and Run and Culpable Homicide, where a white male Rhodes University student was driving his vehicle in Grahamstown and knocked down a black student. He ran away and was traced and arrested and charged. He told me that there was a meeting of three white investigators and a white prosecutor. After that meeting, the charges against that white male were withdrawn and no-one was charged, although there enough evidence that the death of the black student was a result of that accident.

They told me that there is a conspiracy between white police and white prosecutors to create cases against black and coloured police and it is easy to charge a black or coloured person for cases that do not exist. But real cases are covered up for white people.

Their story corroborated what happened to me, where I was charged and prosecuted for a case that never had a complainant and no case was opened against me.

CHAPTER SEVENTEEN

Interview of former Constable Hofman

FORMER CONSTABLE THEO HOFFMAN VISITED me and told me that he lost his police job as a result of a false case opened against him by his former girlfriend on allegations of kidnapping and assault GBH. He was arrested and detained in police cells for eleven months. His former girlfriend came to visit him and informed that she wanted to withdraw the case because she'd never intended to open a case, but her mother forced her to open it because she was angry. The reason was that he normally bought groceries for them, but now he had stopped.

She was told by her mother that if she did not want to open the case, as it was a punishment for him, her mother would chase her from home. She therefore opened the case under duress and that is why she wanted to withdraw. She also on several occasions approached the prosecutor and investigating officer with a request to withdraw the case and make a withdrawal statement, but the prosecutor and investigating officer, who are all white persons, threatened to arrest her if she withdrew the case.

Hofman also told me that his commander, who is a white police colonel, forced him to resign and he indeed wrote a resignation letter and submitted it. After getting legal advice within the same month, he informed his commander that he withdrew the resignation. His commander did not listen to him and processed the resignation. He told me that a Police Regulation called the National Instruction on Service Termination prescribed that, if a police member tendered his or her resignation and decided to withdraw it within the same month, he or she must be allowed to come back.

He told me that the Human Resource section of Grahamstown Police station is headed by white police and they conspired with his commander and made sure that he was not coming back.

Former late Constable Chuman Fiyani also visited me and told me that he was also subjected to Expeditious Process and dismissed in 2021 in Grahamstown, without being afforded a chance to cross examine the witnesses. The chairperson, who was a brigadier, simply called him to a disciplinary hearing and read charges and asked him what he said, and he said he did not do all those allegations of stealing money. That brigadier found him guilty and dismissed him.

He told me that the crimes of many white police officers, who really committed serious crimes, were covered up and the officers are still working in Grahamstown SAPS.

Former Constable Booi also visited me and shared the same painful story. He was subjected to Expeditious Process and dismissed in 2021 for allegations that he posted a comment on Facebook.

Another former Constable Hofman, a coloured female police officer, also visited me and said that there was a case opened in 2017, that she committed fraud on a sick note. Her commander, a white police officer, threatened her by forcing her to resign. She was told that if she did not do that, she would be dismissed. She indeed resigned. After she got legal advice, that one cannot be forced to resign, she approached her commander to reverse resignation. Her commander refused to reverse and processed the resignation and that is how she lost her job.

What happened to these coloured police officers also happened to me. Two white officers in 2011 advised me to resign, but I chased them away.

CHAPTER EIGHTEEN

Interview of Former Sergeant Prince

FORMER SERGEANT PRINCE ALSO VISITED me and narrated his painful story, that he was arrested and charged in a false case and found not guilty in terms of Section 174 and was subjected to Expeditious Process and dismissed by a brigadier. He said many black and coloured people were prosecuted.

As I was used to represent many SAPS members in disciplinary hearings and arbitrations, they requested me to help them by drafting court papers to challenge the constitutionality of their dismissal and to obtain a declaratory order that will declare those regulations unlawful and unconstitutional. I did it because I was also about to be charged and an investigation against me was under way.

NOTICE OF MOTION

IN THE HIGH   COURT OF SOUTH AFRICA

GRAHAMSTOWN EASTERN CAPE

CASE NO 888/2021

IN THE MATTER BETWEEN:

LESLEY SAULS   First Applicant

GARETH PAUL PRINCE   Second Applicant

ANDRE BROWN   Third Applicant

and

MINISTER OF SAFETY AND SECURITY   First Respondent

THE NATIONAL COMMISSOINER OF THE

SOUTH AFRICAN POLICE SERVICE   Second Respondent

NOTICE OF MOTION

KINDLY TAKE NOTICE THAT on a date and on a time to be arranged by the Register, applicants intend to apply to this Honourable Court for an order in the following terms:

1. Declaring unconstitutional and invalid and setting aside regulation 9 of the South African Police regulations , 2016 that was added to normal disciplinary regulations , issued in terms of section 24(1) of the South African Police Act , 1995
2. Declaring unconstitutional and invalid the same regulation 9 as it used by South African Police service to dismiss employees without trial in contravention of section 35(3) (i) of the Constitution .
3. Ordering the Respondent to pay the costs of this application, only if she or he opposes it.

4. Granting the applicant further and or alternative relief.

TAKE NOTICE FURTHER that , the affidavits of the Applicants, Lesley Sauls and supporting affidavit of Gareth Paul Prince and Andre Brown there to, will be used in support of this application.

TAKE NOTICE FURTHER that , the applicants has appointed the following address as address of accepting correspondence and service of documents, no 1 Middle Terrance, Grahamstown , 6139 and e mail address is lestoya14@gmail.com   - telephone 0848655704.

TAKE NOTICE FURTHER that should you intend opposing this application you are required to notify the Applicant in writing within 15 (fifteen) court days of the service of this application on you;

CHAPTER NINETEEN

Affidavit of Former Sergeant Sauls

I DRAFTED A FOUNDING AFFIDAVIT for Lesley Sauls and I was also still on the list to be dismissed. The affidavit reads as follows:

On the 1st of November 2016 the First and Second Respondent published and issued the South African Police Disciplinary Regulations and in addition to those normal disciplinary regulations, they included a special clause that seeks to dismiss every South African Police Member without trial, if they are accused of certain departmental charges listed on Regulation 9.

Those Regulations were called Regulation 9 Expeditious Process and the specific misconduct charges were listed as follows: Aiding an escapee, Arson, Robbery, Assault GBH, Bribery, Corruption, Dealing in Drugs, Defeating the ends of Justice, Extortion, Forgery and Uttering, Fraud, Hijacking, Housebreaking and Theft, Kidnapping, Malicious Damage to Property of a Serious Nature, Murder, Rape, Terrorism, Theft and Sexual Harassment.

On the 13th of October 2019 I was on duty with Constable Freeman when I visited an accident scene.

A South African Breweries truck was involved and the beer was scattered all over. We loaded the beers into the police bakkie for the purpose of safe keeping at the police station. On the way to the police station, I stopped at Mandise Tavern to buy food, as they are selling food. In that process I was arrested, together with Constable Freeman, and charged with theft of liquor.

On the 28th of January 2021, I was subjected to Expeditious Process and charged on seven counts as follows Regulations 5(3) (a) (b) (I) (u) (t) in that I and Constable Freeman stole liquor and sold it to Mandisa Tavern in Joza, Grahamstown, on the 13th of October 2019 and therefore we were charged for theft.

During the day of the trial I appeared and the brigadier who was the chairperson only read the charges as mentioned above and asked me whether I understand the charges and what my plea was. I pleaded not guilty. That brigadier, without any evidence being presented, simply pronounced sanction of dismissal and reported it to the office of the Provincial Commissioner. The office the Provincial Commissioner endorsed the dismissal and dismissed me.

It is my respectful submission that my dismissal is unconstitutional and unlawful and in violation of my constitutional rights, particularly Section 35 (3)(i) of the Constitution, 1996 that says: every accused person has a right to fair trial which includes a right to adduce and challenge evidence against him.

It is further my respectful submission that the actions of the First and Second Respondents did not only violate my constitutional rights, but also the provisions of the Labour Relations Act, 1995, particularly Schedule 8 that deals with substantive and procedural fairness.

The First and Second Respondents denied any wrongdoing in their answering affidavit.

After filing the affidavit, I released a statement in the Daily Despatch:

Fired cops take to Makhanda court over 'unconstitutional' regulation

ASANDA NINI

CHIEF REPORTER

asandan@dispatch.co.za

Three axed Eastern Cape police officers have challenged what they claim is an "unconstitutional" 2016 SAPS regulation that allows the top brass to summarily fire employees without any form of disciplinary process or trial.

The trio last week approached the high court in Makhanda for it to declare Regulation 9 of the SA Police Service discipline regulations as unconstitutional and invalid, and to set it aside.

It was issued by then police minister Nathi Nhleko in 2016.

The regulation is commonly known as the "expeditious process".

In their court papers filed on March 24, the former officers claim the "unconstitutional" regulation has led to a number of police officers accused of transgressions being unfairly dismissed without a hearing or a trial, or the chance to question witnesses or evidence presented against them.

The trio claim only black or coloured police officers in the Makhanda area have fallen victim to the regulation, with many losing their jobs in the process.

They claim their white colleagues received only slaps on the wrist and were still at work.

Former officers Lesley Sauls, Gareth Paul Prince and Adre Brown, the applicants in the matter, claim they were fired without proper disciplinary processes being followed or the opportunity to interrogate witnesses or evidence presented against them.

Cited as respondents are police minister Bheki Cele and national police commissioner Gen Khehla Sitole.

Cele's spokesperson, Lirandzu Themba, on Wednesday confirmed that the matter had been brought to the attention of the minister's office.

She declined to comment on the racism claims.

"Yes, the ministry of police is aware of the court action and it will be opposed.

"Court papers are yet to be filed, so I cannot expand further

They have since written to President Cyril Ramaphosa's office asking him to intervene

on the rest of your questions," said Themba.

Speaking on behalf of the three officers, Sauls on Wednesday said the regulation was being used to persecute black and coloured officers in the Makhanda area, while white officers who had allegedly committed serious crimes were treated with "kid gloves" and still remained in the system.

Sauls was fired on February 8 after he was accused of stealing beer from a truck that had overturned near Makhanda a few years back.

He said he was fired internally, while his criminal case was still ongoing in court.

"If a white official is alleged to have committed a serious offence there will be no DC hearing," Sauls said.

However, he said a black or coloured officer would "be made to appear before a brigadier, who will simply read you the charges, and if he or she is of the view that you did commit such offence, he or she will dismiss you from work without giving you a chance to even cross-examine witnesses".

"You will be dismissed solely on hearsay evidence which you cannot even interrogate."

The three officers provided the Dispatch with a list of white officers whom they claim had found themselves on the wrong side of the law but had not been dismissed.

They have since written to President Cyril Ramaphosa's office asking him to intervene in what they term "gross racism" at their workplace.

In their memo to Ramaphosa, they say cases are being "planted" against non-white officers, leading to their unfair dismissal.

Ramaphosa's acting spokesperson, Tyrone Seale, could not be reached for comment on Wednesday.